Reflections

from a small town

newspaper columns from the 1950s

Gerald Barry

Edited by Margaret Barry

Dear Betty,

I hope you enjoy fond memories of Groton.

Love,
Margaret

Reflections from a small town

Newspaper columns from the 1950s

Gerald Barry

Edited by Margaret Barry

First printing 2000

Printed in the United States of America

ISBN 009654447-8-3   One Big Pr.

Library of Congress Control Number 00-091916

Distributed by

Margaret Barry

PO Box 18362

Rochester, NY 14681 – 0362

e-mail   magbarry@rochester.rr.com

This book is published to honor my parents,
Marion and Gerald Barry.

♪

The original columns did not have titles or photographs.

The first section on family is arranged in chronological order of generations. The date of the column is listed with each column.

The second and third sections are arranged in chronological order of publication.

♪ = Editor's note

Acknowledgements

♪

I am thankful for the generosity and encouragement of my family and friends. Cindy Ahrens produced the second draft with loving precision. Lisa and Kris Schneider patiently guided my computer travails and rescued the cover, text, photos, and me, on numerous occasions. Grandson Griffin is the reason I bought a computer in the first place. Tom Barry worked heroically against sinister software on layout and design when he already had too many other responsibilities. David Barry, Ann Owens, and Judith T. Montello gave thoughtful suggestions and tender support. Jean True, Mart and Gary Smith were colorful sources of Groton information. Kathleen Vetrano was a cheerful source of colorful family information.

A tribute to Gerald Barry

Hushang Bahar, the first president of Tompkins-Cortland Community College, wrote this tribute to Gerald in the issue of the college paper following Gerald's death in 1968. Gerald had written three issues of "The Communicator" as part of what was to be his public relations position at the college after he completed his work at SCM.

"You rarely meet a man with whom you become totally involved, whose very existence leaves a great impact on yours. Gerald Barry was such a man whose name you, the readers, never found anywhere on the pages of the "Communicator." He came to our lives very late, for we have known him only a few months, and he left us very early for he died in an automobile accident: a cruel and senseless way to die.

Our college and his colleagues will continue the "Communicator" in his name and memory and with his touch of love and passion for humanity.

We shall remember Gerry always, for his presence was a breath of fresh air in a terribly polluted world.

Wherever you turn in Groton, you see reflections of him. Over at the Smith-Corona plant across the street from the college you talk to people who knew him when he was in charge of Personnel, or when he was editor of the company publication, the Keyboard, written in his own warm and personal style. Stop in at the busy Groton Library where he was an active Board member for years. He was a charter member of the Finger Lakes Library Board and brought Groton into that system.

Or walk over to the Municipal Swimming Pool, something he helped bring to this village of 2,500. Drive by the modern elementary or secondary schools on your way out to the new Groton Golf Course and Club House. Gerry worked long and hard to encourage the villagers to plan and complete all these projects – through his newspaper column and through his own active and enthusiastic support, time, and effort. He was instrumental in bringing this new Community College to Groton and helped make it a welcoming place for the students and faculty.

How did he accomplish all he did – all the tangibles, all the intangibles that add up to spirit of community? Why did he stay in Groton? Why did he get so involved in the life of the community? Following his column "Reflections" over the course of the ten years it appeared in the "Groton Journal and Courier" will give you some of the answers. You will know more about a man with a wide range of interests, with a gentle humor, with firm and sensitive faith in human beings. His columns are personal essays – a form of writing which is virtually a lost art in an age of anonymity and group authorship. His essays are personal responses to a wide range of events, from summers on his grandfather's farm, to "The Vandals" band, to this small town.

He was a skilled musician, writer, photographer, and he was largely self-taught. He was an activist, a worker, and an inspiration to those who knew him. His life was truly a celebration of life."

Family

Gerald Barry, 1916

"On this day let us know family peace.

Bind us anew to one another.

Open our eyes to the miracles we are

And to the gifts we've been given.

And having found peace in the little world of our
    family,

Lead us, family by family, to the larger promise

Of peace on earth to men of good will."

Lucy Morgan McCormick, 1843-1926, and George McCormick, 1832-1927. Both were born in County Louth, Ireland.

Saint Patrick's Day in the mornin'. . . Killarney's in the air . . . there's much Wearin' of the Green and I find myself thinking of two real jewels of Erin, George and Lucy McCormick. She was a quiet, gentle, great-hearted woman. Her blue-gray eyes showed at once the sadness and the gaiety which the Irish so readily express. He was as blustery as a summer storm, a paycock of a man who amused himself and his neighbors by fighting half his life over a fence line "just for the principle of the thing."

She could say more in two words and a look than he could in an afternoon. Yet there was a fine understanding between them. They complemented each other and put into their lives the simple, absolute faith two people need to live 65 years of devotion to each other.

They were "Grandpa" and "Grandma" to me. "Turncoat," he'd shout when I climbed in the car to leave his farm before summer vacation was over. "Turncoat runnin' back to your ma," and everyone would laugh — but me. I remember her best standing in the pantry door. She watched for me when I came riding in on a load of hay with my Uncle Art. She'd motion me to the house to have a huge slice of homemade bread and butter with sugar sprinkled on top, or a glass of milk and a cookie "to keep up my strength." On a hot day, she'd send me into the field with a quart can of boiled cider. "Let your grandfather drink first," she'd warn me. "He'll not drink after that tobacco-chewin' hired man."

My grandmother was as American as a Grant Wood painting. She put her roots down deeply and finally in her adopted land. My grandfather lived on magnified memories of County Dowd and Blackrock, and his service to Lord Claremont of Hagerstown Castle. When he became too expansive, as he frequently did with company at his mercy, my grandmother would quiet him with a "Pshaw" and a look that said, "George McCormick, where in all Ireland could you have owned a farm like this and set a table for twenty people with no thought but to stuff them with your vittles and your blather."

After a few silent mouthfuls, my grandfather would start in all over again, but quietly, at his end of the table. "I remember the time . . ." he'd begin in a confidential stage whisper. Most likely he'd tell how many stone of wheat he'd carried to win first prize at Clonakilty Fair. He'd tell it straight and nobody laughed if he added a couple of stone to recoup his lost prestige.

With all the loquacious Irishmen that surely have reached heaven by now, Saint Patrick must be a harried man. "This is no bad place at all," I can hear my grandfather tell him, "but not to be compared in many ways to Blackrock. Did I ever tell you of the time I drove Lord Claremont's rig from Dundalk to Ballybay?"

St. Patrick must be grateful that Lucy McCormick is there, ready with a quiet "Pshaw" and a meaningful look to keep one imaginative Irishman in line.

My grandfather looked like a sea captain. His whiskers grew up out of his collar and underscored an already forceful jaw. He had bright, blue eyes and even when he was past 90, stooped and dependent on a cane, he somehow gave the impression of being straight as a ramrod and just as inflexible about his wants.

As long as he was able, he ran his farm like a three-masted schooner racing before a big wind. But as he grew older and more of the hard work fell to his sons and daughters, he became a sort of honorary advisor on farm and family matters — often unheeded but never unheard.

My branch of the family were town folks. Although our pilgrimages to the farm were frequent and fruitful, grandfather rarely returned a visit. One summer, prompted by the acquisition of a new automobile, an immense Buick touring car which appealed to his Irish vanity, he allowed himself to be driven to our town for a few visits.

The various branches of the family would hardly finish the first round of conversation before grandfather would announce that he was ready to go home. The first two times the visits were cut short according to his wishes, but the third time one of my aunts stumbled on the reason for grandpa's anxiety. She found him searching in vain in the back of our house and realized at once the old man's predicament. She told him that our place was equipped with inside conveniences. This brought a roar of protest.

"I never did the likes in a man's house yet," he stormed, "and I'm not going to start now." He underscored this announcement with an imperious wave of his cane. There was nothing to do but take grandpa home to the peace and propriety of country life.

Children of Lucy and John McCormick

Name	Dates	Birthplace	Pages
John	1868-1955	born in Ireland	
Arthur	1871-1929	born on ship to US	pp. 19-24, 25-31
Bernard	1874-1903	Born in Scipio, NY	
Margaret	1877-1956	"	pp. 40-42, 53-57
Ann	1880-1956	"	pp. 19-24
Mary (Sister Anastasia)	1882-1976	"	pp. 32-39
Lucy	1885-1969	"	

Children of Ellen Walpole Barry, 1837-1894, and Thomas Barry, 1825 - 1891. Both were born in County Cork, Ireland.

Name	Dates	Birthplace	Pages
Mary	1866-1895		
James	1867-1928		
Ellen	1870-1930		
Elizabeth	1871-1897		
Tom	1875-1940		
John	1875-1940	Born in "North Ireland", Groton	pp. 40-42, 43-48
Daniel	1877-1929		

"Outa there, Bub," my Uncle Art called to me as he passed the big feed bin on his way to the horse barn to hitch up the team. I was trying to hide in the bin from Brownie, the McCormick farm dog who was my only summer companion, and an obliging and intelligent one at that.

No one else ever called me Bub. It was a commonplace enough name but it sounded warm and special to me whenever Uncle Art said it, often as not leaving the rest of whatever he had on his mind unexpressed. It was one of the few things that came to his lips readily. When I was seven and sent to my grandfather's farm for the summer, Uncle Art seemed a big man to me but actually he wasn't very tall. His shoulders were heavy, rounded and powerful. His hands were wide with thick fingers that were forever letting nuts slip through them or getting pinched and bruised — fingers that were made for gripping a pick and shovel or plow handles.

There was hardly a graceful thing about him. He walked heavily, taking three or four steps straight and then lurching slightly to the side to catch his balance. His face was plain enough and yet there was a presence about him. His hair was reddish but no match for mine. Redder than his hair was his moustache and he continually rubbed it as if to reassure himself that it was still there.

Uncle Art's eyes were light blue. They seemed to look out on the world as if imprisoned behind them was a lively and fanciful spirit that wanted to be freed from an awkward body but knew that escape was impossible — well, almost impossible.

Uncle Art's great strengths were physical and — I came to appreciate much later — spiritual. He was no mental giant. Indeed he didn't need to be. His sister, my Aunt Ann, was ready to plan for him and anyone else who came within her orbit.

She was and still is a "Good Woman" with all the terrifying attributes that "Good Women" sometimes have. Aunt Ann was bent on firming up my character during the summer months when she had me, a somewhat unmalleable putty, in her hands.

When Aunt Ann meant business, which was nearly all the time, she simply called me, "Boy," a term I resented.. When she said, "Now just a minute, Boy," she was plainly addressing an inferior creature. "Boy" was a challenge which brought out her best. Man power and horse power did not escape her managerial talents which were considerable. But she was the most efficient user of boy power I've ever known. Even her apparent lapses were thoroughly planned. When I was old enough to help turn the churn, she would take over at the critical point and say, "Well, go swing awhile." After possibly five minutes of pumping idly under the maples in the front yard, of kicking into the mulberry bush and teasing Brownie with a short piece of rope tied to one shoe, the mailman would come along with the morning *Post Standard* and I would find myself running into the house with the mail and back into Aunt Ann's regimen. "Well, Boy," she'd say as she handed grandfather the paper, "I guess it's about time you got to pickin' those sour cherries."

Cutting the hay, harvesting the wheat, selling a calf — the whole farm was Aunt Ann's province. And the big red barns that stood on the McCormick acres were monuments to her determination and shrewdness and to Uncle Art's hard labor and her own. She made the weight of her decisions felt in all directions. And she never neglected the work in the house. The washing, churning, cooking, marketing, and cleaning were swiftly done. Sickness, when it came finally to my grandfather and grandmother, she managed with the same authority she'd exercise on a drinking hired man. About the only disease she ever really bowed to was old age — and she fought even that relentlessly.

"She's a horse for work," more than one hired man said. And she was a horse who kept a weather eye out to see that no one else slacked off in the traces. Not that Uncle Art was ever found wanting but his "Bub" who liked to swing under the maples and look at the stereopticon in the front parlor and visit the Batzers across the road — folks who never seemed to have much work to do and who even read books in the middle of haying — he could stand some attention. And while summer lasted and the endless chores on the farm supplied Aunt Ann with the opportunity for developing his character, he got it.

"Get those shoulders back, Boy," Aunt Ann charged me when I came into her kitchen with a few eggs discovered, likely as not, many days too late in the old horse barn. "Just you look at cousin Art Morgan the next time he comes out to the farm. Straight as a fork handle, that man. You could do worse than grow up like him."

To Aunt Ann a man's shoes were a revealing indication of moral worth. "Look at a man's heels," she'd say and at the same time take a scathing look at mine. "You can tell a lot about a man by looking at his heels."

Another major issue between us was my left-handedness which Aunt Ann regarded exactly as she did dirty feet — simply not to be tolerated. My mother was enlightened enough to accept left-handedness for what it was — a certain awkwardness that might be compensated for later in the pitcher's box or at first base. Besides, in bringing only one left-hander in seven into the world she felt, and rightly enough, that she had done all any reasonable person could have demanded.

But Aunt Ann wasn't reasonable about a good many things. She admonished me never to drink root beer because there was a link, she was sure, between root and real beer that never in my life should be forged. Vinegar was another untouchable. I could have lettuce with milk and sugar on it or beans with her own chili sauce. But no vinegar. There was a danger in cultivating an appetite for strong drink.

And so I ate with my right hand and shined my heels and stood up straight or received a warning about the lack of self-discipline that was countenanced in the flesh pots of Groton. (And though I don't stand up very straight these days or pay special heed to my heels, I use my right hand with considerable skill for a left-hander.)

But there were brief escapes from the admonitions of a well-meaning aunt. A few days during the summer my grandfather wasn't equal to drawing the milk to Venice Center. If the farm work was held up by rain, Uncle Art might clap me on the head and toss me roughly up on the seat of his democrat wagon and take me "to town" with him.

It would be a quiet journey. Grandpa was a born conversationalist who thought that other folks were just naturally-born listeners. But Uncle Art would sit beside me and squint his watery blue eyes and think about all the work to be done as soon as we got back home. He would like to have talked, I'm sure, but as we passed a rig going in the opposite direction, all he could manage was a polite "Mornin'." If the other rig drew up for a more lengthy exchange, Uncle Art might venture to say, "Well, it might clear up by night, as a feller says," or, "No use complainin', as a feller says." And he was ready to move on.

If our trip was made at the end of summer and he felt maybe a twinge of loneliness at the long winter months ahead, we might wait a few minutes so I could see the Shortline blaze by on its way to Ithaca. Then we'd stop at the Venice Center store and Uncle Art would postpone his real purpose for coming and let me squirm over the candy counter and look longingly at the cases of pop. After awhile he'd say, "Bub?"

I'd look at him impishly and ask, "Root beer?"

"Well now," he'd say and rub his moustache and deliberate on a problem usually settled at a higher level. "Well now, I guess that'll go for me too." I never supposed that I enjoyed mine any more than Uncle Art did his.

As we drove toward home, he began to be impatient to get back to mending fences or sharpening the knives on the cutter bar of his cussed binder and he bent forward and slapped the lines uneasily on the horses' rumps. When we turned the corner that brought us close to the driveway of the McCormick farm, Uncle Art looked at me as if to confirm the pact between us. He left all the details of a gentlemen's agreement unsaid but completely understood.

That noon I forced myself to an extra helping of potatoes, sat up straight in my chair and used my right hand exclusively. After he pushed back from the table, Uncle Art put his hand on my head and said, "Goin' home Sunday, Bub . . ." And he paused a minute and rested his great hands on the door frame and looked at the shadowy front lawn where I loved to play and where he rarely had time to sit. Then he pushed his awkward frame through the doorway and walked his slow, steady gait to the barn.

What other secrets did that quiet man keep, I wonder, besides having root beer in Venice Center?

My uncle, Art McCormick, was a farmer. This may be too all-inclusive a description because "farmer" to you may mean the college-educated, technical-minded manager demanded by today's mechanistic tilling of the earth. Uncle Art would have been happier if he had been born thousands of years earlier. He could have handled a stone hoe or a crude plow. He was that kind of a farmer. No tractor or combine for him. He lived long enough to see the revolution coming and such equipment as he had, mowing machine, side rake, hay loader, binder, bedeviled him and frustrated him.

Everything about him was thick — his fingers, his wrists, his shoulders and neck. And to be brutally honest, he was a bit thick in the head over a good many things that an ordinary man does easily and without thinking. He was built for heavy work and that was what he enjoyed most. He could plow and dig post holes and pull stumps with any man, but with a wrench in his hand he was destruction itself. To describe him fully would be to say, as well, that he had a great heart. And as between head and heart, if a man must have a shortcoming in one place or the other, let it be in his head.

All his life Uncle Art had a running fight with a grain binder, a machine that transcended his comprehension as much as a digital computer transcends mine. The binder was never quite up to tying all the bundles. As long as only an occasional bundle was skipped, my grandfather rather enjoyed following along behind to make up for the binder's mechanical shortcomings. He would pick up a wisp of wheat in each hand, knot them together, secure them around the bundle in a fashion that I'm sure he felt was the way God had intended wheat to be tied. If the binder acted up too seriously, the old gentleman would straighten up from his task and point out to me that he could probably cradle the lot of it, tie it and shock it in less time than that quixotic contraption – if they'd only let him.

The binder must have stood still in the field at least as much as it ever ran. I can remember catching up to it as I helped my grandfather shock the bundles. Uncle Art would be reaching down inside with a wrench. His blue eyes were troubled as he pushed his head into the maze of levers and rods and fingers to try to determine what to twist, what to yank or pound to beat the binder into submission.

The longer he worked, the more impatient and confused he got. In exasperation he would pull too hard on the wrench and strip a nut or twist a bolt right off.

Tractors became commonplace on the farms around but Uncle Art stuck to his horses. Four wheels and two horses was all the machinery he cared to cope with. As the roads improved, the McCormick clan yielded to progress enough to experiment with an automobile. An Overland touring car seemed to be so manageable that even Uncle Art was encouraged to learn to operate it. And after a fashion, he succeeded. But it was an uneasy conquest. Being the most expendable hand on the farm, I was detailed to accompany him whenever he went in the car. None of the rest of the family ever came along when Uncle Art was at the wheel. But I was willing, even happy, to risk my neck to get out of weeding carrots or pumping water.

As close as Uncle Art ever came to mastery of the automobile was a Sunday he decided to retrace the trips he made as a younger man with a steam engine threshing outfit. By thinking of the farms where he had stopped with the smoking black engine and the threshing machine, he seemed to relax. We went through Moravia and off into Bear Swamp country, to Auburn and back to his Scipio farm. He considered it a great adventure to have driven so far without one jarring incident.

The following Saturday he hailed me from the horse barn. "Bub, how'd you like to go to Merrifield with me?" he asked. I let go of the barnyard pump in mid-turn. Merrifield! There was a store there with candy and bananas and Boy Scout shoes. We had to take milk to the creamery, stop at the store and − well, the barnyard watering trough wasn't even quarter-full. Perhaps Uncle Art's happy experience of the week before gave him the illusion that he was a driver. He let the clutch out as abruptly as he'd trip a hayfork. The Overland lurched, bucked and stopped dead still. It started again and when he succeeded, he drove out of the yard a shaken man.

When we started west down the dirt road toward Merrifield, I knew Uncle Art had had a relapse because he was driving on the left side of the road. He rather liked that side and he seemed to resent the necessity of pulling to the right when another car approached him. One of my duties as a sort of co-pilot was to remind him not to take the brow of a hill on the left side of the road. I let him drive undisturbed for a quarter of a mile but when we approached a slight curve and the start of a gentle slope that would bring up to the State Road, my instinct of self-preservation overruled my reluctance to remind Uncle Art that he just had to pull over to protect, if not himself or me, at least the Overland. He paused at the edge of the State Road, got an all-clear signal from me and shot the Overland across the main highway. Wide ditches filled with water temporarily distracted me from Uncle Art's driving until we came to the bottom of a short but steep hill. Normally, Uncle Art gauged his hills conservatively. If he thought there was any chance he'd have to shift gears midway, he would stop at the bottom of the hill and shift into the gear he was certain would take him over the top.

Once he had made his selection, he would stick to it and, if necessary, would encourage the car by pumping back and forth behind the wheel — and he expected his passenger to do likewise — so he could get over the top without risking the delicate operation of shifting in mid-hill.

He started up the hill to Merrifield in second and I knew before we were halfway that the Overland would never make it. Uncle Art started pumping and he looked at me questioningly to start me pumping too. We were both rocking back and forth in sympathy with the struggling car. Just before the Overland made a last convulsive gasp, Uncle Art jammed in the clutch, yanked the shift lever from second to low, caught the motor, released the clutch and permitted himself a half-smile at pulling off so complicated a maneuver. His arms stiffened at the wheel and he pushed his back into the leather cushion. The motor roared. The snub-nosed little Overland finished off the hill at 10 miles an hour. Before we reached the top, I could see that Uncle Art was thinking that maybe he could master this automobile yet.

Once over the hill, we turned right and drove the remaining two miles to Merrifield. At the milk station the Overland joined the half circle of rigs and automobiles waiting to unload milk. Uncle Art drew up behind a woman in a buggy with one can of milk tied on the back. He managed a half dozen starts and stops until he drove from one door where the cans were taken off to the next where clean cans were picked up. The woman in the buggy failed to start her horse as quickly as Uncle Art expected and he bumped the buggy with the front of the car. The woman's horse reared and started to bolt. An alert farmer leaped from his wagon, grabbed the horse's bridle and calmed the animal. No one tried to calm the woman. Even before she started to talk, Uncle Art's face showed red blotches. His eyes watered and he bit his lips. Women were even more mysterious to him than binders. He couldn't say anything and, indeed, wasn't given a chance to. When the woman finally stopped her harangue, I was relieved for Uncle Art's sake — and my own too because the next stop would be the high point of the journey for me.

When we got back to the Merrifield General store he shoved his big right hand into his pocket. "Here's a dime, Bub," he said. A whole dime! I understood that the trip was to be reported as uneventful. He let me take my time to study the candy counter. I even indulged myself in a package of candy cigarettes which my Aunt Ann hated. But sneaking a candy cigarette was about the only adventure I could think of to make weeding the garden at all interesting.

Finally, Uncle Art put a big hand on my head and twisted it toward the door. "We'd better be gettin' back," he said and I knew he was even more reluctant to start than I was. We headed out of Merrifield, reached the corner, turned and came to the top of the hill. Even with horses, Uncle Art was nervous as he broke over the crest of a steep incline. Whenever we started down Cascade Hill or the Long Hill, he demanded a moment of silence while he sized up the situation and summoned his courage to make the descent.

"Now just be quiet," he always said. He said it again as we stopped on the top of Merrifield Hill.

"Now just be quiet." He was worried by a car parked at the bottom, and it looked to be well into the center of the road. His preoccupation with the other car caused him to let the Overland start rolling in neutral. When he realized he was moving, Uncle Art tried to get the car in gear without using the clutch. There was a horrible clash of gears. Finally the car gained enough momentum so he didn't dare to drive with one hand on the wheel and one hand on the shift knob. He completely forgot about brakes. He yelled at the people in the car at the bottom of the hill. His great hands squeezed the wheel. He hunched ahead numb with fear. I was horrified to be going so fast with Uncle Art. I didn't see how he could get by the car or even keep the Overland in the road if he had it all to himself.

I never knew what happened because I crawled down under the dashboard. I felt the Overland lurch to one side, bound violently, skid and finally straighten out and stop. How Uncle Art managed to miss the other car and keep his own car in the road, I never knew and I'm sure he never did.

When I crawled back up on the seat, Uncle Art was breathing heavily. Perspiration hung in beads on the end of his moustache. He wiped them off, bit his lips and suddenly jutted out his jaw as if he'd come to an irrevocable decision.

He started the car up again, shifted cautiously into low, let the clutch out as gently as he ever managed that baffling operation. The rest of the way home he never changed gears. The radiator was boiling angrily when we crawled into the yard of the McCormick farm. He left the car outside the carriage barn and went to the horse stable and was sick to his stomach.

I rode a good many times with Uncle Art after that but it was always behind a team of horses. He was happier that way—and so was I.

During the summer, the McCormick farm was the prescribed destination for my family. Sometimes there was a picnic on the long tables under the maple trees in the front yard. More often, there was a substantial meal of vittles set out on the oval oak dining room table which seemed to have no limits to its extensibility — certainly none to its hospitality.

Other members of the clan McCormick gathered there also and when Sister Anastasia of the Order of St. Joseph, whom I finally came to understand was my mother's sister, was able to be home for a Sunday, a visit to the farm was an absolute requirement.

Family shoes and manners were freshly polished. Instructions to say, "Yes, Sister," and "No, Sister," when addressing Aunt Mary were passed down the family ranks until a man near the bottom was known to have absentmindedly responded to his astonished teacher, "Yes, Sister . . . I mean, Miss Hutchins."

At the farm, all of us children faced detailed inquiries. Progress was expected and Sister Anastasia, nurse, Hospital Superintendent, school teacher, had, for a woman who had forsaken all worldly interests and goods, a surprising knowledge of worldly goings-on.

"So we're studying South America," she'd say to one of us in the sixth grade. "Now where would we find a famous Statue of Christ?"

"And here's a young gentleman who can write his name?" And the young gentleman had to produce evidence to support the claim advanced for him. She was always keen to know what we were being taught in science to see if any ungodly dogmas could be detected in our answers. There were pointed inquiries into which young men the girls were going with. "And what's this I hear about bobbed hair?" She had an astounding range of interests and information.

Once I contributed unwittingly to her worldly education when she visited our home on Clark Street soon after we had acquired our first Victrola. My mother, who had a good many more important things to do than operate the new machine, had to call me in from across the street at Griffins to demonstrate the latest family acquisition. As I wound up the machine, I deliberated over what record to play. The choice was rather limited but I could have made a successful debut as a disc jockey and selected the only Red Seal Victor 12 inch record we owned, Alma Gluck singing "Carry Me Back to Old Virginia." It was our only claim to recorded culture but I passed it by for one that I thought would bring down the house, "Mr. Gallagher and Mr. Shean."

Somehow, with Sister Anastasia sitting in the room, the record didn't seem funny at all. In the middle of the record, Mr. Shean asked an embarrassing question which I no longer remember. When Mr. Gallagher replied, "In the bathroom, Mr. Shean," I was told, "Please let's not hear any more of THAT." And I sheepishly shut off the Victrola. During the years that followed I was more circumspect in choosing Aunt Mary's entertainment.

By the time I was a freshman in high school I was aware of a division in family interest. The visits to the McCormick farm, the promise of a ham dinner with milk gravy, beet greens, new potatoes, sweet corn and green apple pie, in addition to a supper of more ham, creamed potatoes, Columbia berries and whipped cream cake — bounteous as it all was — interfered with following the destiny of the Corona baseball team.

One of Sister Anastasia's visits coincided, unfortunately, with a critical game at Cortland. My father had not only a sportsman's interest but a healthy financial stake in the outcome of the game. The remaining menfolk in the family, all save one now in long pants, were equally involved. And once the umpire yelled, "Play Ball," my mother was the most rabid fan of all.

For this particular Sunday a compromise was arranged whereby a morning visit to the farm and an early dinner would allow the family to be excused in time to get to the ball game.

Instead of her customary one companion, three nuns accompanied Sister Anastasia. They were less talkative, I noticed, than the sisters she usually brought to the farm. Some of those nuns were truly lively and witty, delightful conversationalists. My grandfather was at his most grandiloquent in the presence "of the cloth." And my grandmother was quietly proud of the family gathered round her and the fine table of vittles she set.

During the customary inquiries into "what we were taking," Paul reported that he was in fifth grade and his teacher, Miss Price, had taught every one of the Barrys. "Well, she's earned her place in Heaven," Aunt Mary said. "And Mr. High School Freshman in long pants," she inquired, turning to me, "you must be quite a Latin scholar by now?" Before I could prove this by declining "agricola," someone who lacked confidence in my Latin interceded by saying I had been in a speaking contest.

I shriveled up inside at the prospect of what I feared faced me. Long after that ordeal in the Groton Opera House I still found myself dreaming of forgetting my lines. My reaction to the contest — which was really a contest against achieving perfection, or at least Maude Cody Burnham's idea of perfection — was never to utter a word of my "piece" again. However, a more determined mind than mine immediately programmed the declamation as an after dinner treat.

Not the least important of Sister Anastasia's vows was the one of obedience. She vowed it for herself and extended it to a considerable degree to include the relationship of nephews and nieces to her. When she decided to program my speaking contest piece as an after dinner treat, even though the family wanted to get away for a critical baseball game at Cortland, I sulked. And I was a skilled sulker. I even cried a little, most undignified for a high school freshman, at the thought of having to dredge up out of my mind page after page of *The Last Full Measure of Devotion* for a far more critical audience than the one I had faced in the Groton Opera House.

After dinner, I held out stubbornly while the dishes were cleared away but when the pronouncement came, with the authority of a Papal Bull behind it, that no one would leave for the baseball game until I had delivered the piece, I was immediately subjected to remorseless pressure from my father and brothers. They consulted watches and estimated how many innings this conflict was going to cost them.

"The sooner you get it over with, the sooner we can go," they told me resignedly.

I finally gave in, blew my nose and started. At the beginning, habit took over. I relaxed my arms at my sides, stood straighter than usual with my shoulders back so far that Aunt Ann nodded approvingly, took a deep breath, held my head up, placed my feet slightly apart with toes pointed the least bit out. It was all as automatic as a pilot's pre-flight check-off. There were no half-way measures in Maude Cody Burnham's directions.

The three visiting nuns, my aunts and uncles, grandfather and grandmother and my family arranged themselves around one end of the dining room table and along a brown leather couch usually reserved for my grandfather's afternoon nap. I stood at the opposite end of the room where the wood burning stove was placed during the winter and began:

"He could not bear sitting on the porch any longer; he got up and went to the dining room door."

"Supper late, Mama?"

I tried to lower the pitch of my voice to indicate that a 50-year-old man was speaking. But the first part of "Mama" and the second part must have been separated by a spread of two octaves. I was off to a shaky start.

"Just a few minutes. Take your paper back to the porch, Papa. I'll call you."

The hands came up from my sides and joined in a feminine gesture of anguish and desperation . . . at the same time, a slight turn to the left to indicate more fully another character . . . shoulders hunched slightly . . . voice softened and raised.

At least I was airborne, somewhat shakily, but I began to see the paragraphs coming ahead, even the penciled notations . . . "HUNDRED" written in large letters at the top of the second page and underscored by Mrs. Burnham to blot out that elocutionist's horror "hunderd."

After the first bit of conversation, the story of *The Last Full Measure of Devotion* was sketched quickly . A father and mother who kept from each other for a week the tragic knowledge of a son lost in World War I. The pathos was real enough and delivered to people conditioned to accept speaking contest behaviour as genuinely moving no matter how ridiculous it might seem now.

"Young Steve Morrow wanted to enlist and fight with the Canadians . . . Then came May of 1915, with its world-stabbing horror to show how a nation may, having once lost her soul . . ."

The right hand was up, voice stern and driving. The relatives were properly moved. Handkerchiefs were at the ready. Pride shone through the tears. Sister Anastasia beamed with cautious pride at her nephew's delivery. But the other nuns, I noticed, sat stony-faced at even the most emotional passages.

Finally toward the end . . . hands clasped again . . . and wringing . . . A dramatic pause for emphasis . . . Then in an emotion-choked voice:

"Supper's ready, Papa." He got a smile ready for his lips, and went in. She had a smile to meet his. He had taken his seat before he noticed the content of a big platter before his plate.

Hands outspread . . . Alarm, confusion . . . A breathy, choked "Why, why beefsteak pie? Why I thought . . ."

And the struggle to keep the bitter news was over. Steve's favorite dish, not to be served until he came home from the war . . . Then it was that the first grief-softening tears came to Mr. Morrow's eyes . . . Tears of pride and love as well.

With the last words came a few seconds hold so as not to break the spell so laboriously created. Then a slight bow of the head and it was over.

The quiet and the spell were immediately shattered by the roar of the motor on our 1925 Maxwell and I piled into the car and headed for Cortland with my family — restored to the good graces of the Clan McCormick.

On our next visit to the farm I overheard some expressions of regret that everyone had been so insistent on my delivering the prize speaking piece anyway. The three visiting nuns were recent arrivals from Germany and not at all warmed by the impassioned references to their countrymen.

There was cruel justice to all this I felt. Those pages and pages of printed words, under-scorings, and marginal notations I restored to a warm place in my heart. I had given my "last full measure of devotion" to put-upon nephews everywhere.

"Born in a hotel room and, dammit, died in one."
So said playwright Eugene O'Neil in delirium and
bitterness at the end of his life. He was leaving not so
much his Pulitzer prizes and major works in the
American theatre as his unfinished cycle of plays and
enough notebooks full of sketches to keep him writing
for another lifetime. But he came full cycle and saw
the bitter pattern of his own life as clearly as he
created a character in one of his plays.

Last summer I spent a quiet vacation in Groton. I
took pictures of most of the houses that were part of
Gripp's *Historical Souvenir* and Marion and I went on
a few long and leisurely walks. One noon we started
up Clark Street, stopped in both cemeteries; then
walked north to Howe's Corners; turned west to the
Country Grill and south along the Locke-Groton Road.

When we came to Walpole Road I decided to take a
picture of the house where I was born. Across the
bridge, took another picture of the little house where
my family started. "North Ireland," my father called
it. A few steps further on we came to the railroad
crossing and decided to walk up the tracks to town.
This is the part of the journey that I've made over and
over again. Halfway, we stopped and talked with Art
Walpole who was mowing a field of hay close to the
tracks. We talked as my family and his family must
have talked a good many times in that same location.

As I walked slowly along the ties and Marion tried
balancing on the track, I tried to get the feeling my
grandfather must have had as he hurried to town
along the rails in the early spring with a whole season

Harold	Madalene	George	Bernardine	John
1898-1973	1900-1983	1902-1981	1903-1945	1905-1979

Gerald	Margaret McCormick Barry and John Barry		Paul
1911-1968	1877-1956	1876-1953	1916-1999

of ditch digging and gardening ahead of him. I could see my dad and uncles trying to make headway back to North Ireland after a riotous visit in town . . . the ties in all the wrong places . . . the rails expanding and contracting in a devilish pattern . . . and the road bed altogether too narrow for spraddle-footed Irishmen in their cups.

And I could see, too, a strong young woman with reddish hair, a determined chin, body bending into a biting morning wind, frequently looking back to the little house with a deep hurt in her eyes, fighting against an overpowering maternal instinct — a struggle so many women know today — against leaving a houseful of red-headed youngsters to take care of themselves while she did housework in town.

Marion and I left the tracks at the lumber yard; crossed the bridge; walked up the bank steps, down Main Street, and home. This was the journey then. For my dad there was perhaps "too much of the battle cry and the bottle cry." And yet he was given the grace to live the last ten years of his life in serenity and security. For my mother, was there too much of the tigress protecting her young? Oh, there was some of this, yet she instinctively understood more about people than has yet been put between the covers of a good many books. They were salt pork and milk gravy Irish; mush and milk and fried potatoes Irish; eat the chicken or have the eggs Irish; scrapple and oatmeal and home made bread; and always, tea, tea, tea.

They moved to town, to Clark Street, to Lincoln Avenue, to Barrows Street, to East South Street and then the final journey up to Clark Street cemetery. Born in Groton; died in Groton. True of my father; true in a sense of my mother for she was born not forty miles away. And as I look along the shelf of Irish writers, to Yeats, O'Casey, Joyce, O'Connor, none of them tells me more of the Irish or more of myself than the journey my mother and father made up the tracks from North Ireland.

The Tombstone for Martin Walpole   September 14, 1950

There's many a worse thing a man could do of a winter evening than to sit down and listen to his father. If the old gentleman has a pipe full of tobacco and a mind full of talk, well, when they're both emptied, you'll be a wiser and he'll be a happier man.

One of my dad's favorite tales — and there may be better ones to be told in this valley and you're welcome to tell them here any week you feel inclined—is of the tombstone his father carved with a cold chisel for Martin Walpole.

I've no very clear picture of my grandfather, Tom Barry. He wasn't too tall a man but he had a rugged body and a rugged spirit. He also had a fiery red full beard and a disposition, when the occasion arose, to match it. He was no great drinkin' man but when he'd dug a ditch as straight and fair as any ditch in these parts was ever dug, he'd clean out the dirt in his throat with a glass of ale — and that was that. For a poor devil who lived by the tracks — and the muscles in his back — in a little settlement beyond town called North Ireland, he was a proud man. And that's not a strange thing because you don't have to throw a stone too far even these days to hit a poor but proud Irishman.

As my dad tells it, Martin Walpole lived in a little house across the road from my grandfather. Martin was a lone soul and he and my grandfather were fast friends. When Martin died he was buried in McLean and there seemed to be no one responsible for seeing that his grave was suitably marked.

Without stoppin' to think twice nor repeatin' yourself once, you could probably fill this sheet with the faults of the Irish: Envy and spite . . . but that's another tale altogether. If you were tryin' to fill up a wee corner with their virtues, you might have to stop and think awhile but surely you would have to put down in the end that they have a great, almost mystical respect for their dead. They might even carry it a bit too far for you, but where's the man who thinks he can change that.

Tom Barry couldn't sleep nights for thinking of Martin's grave unmarked so he had a piece of stone quarried from John Walpole's farm and he set to work chinking out the letters with a cold chisel. Leisure was no problem in those days and a man was lucky if he had 10 minutes to spare of an evenin' after he'd put in a 10-hour day for 90 cents — and done his chores as well. It took Tom a week to get the name finished. My dad watched him every night and during the day when Tom was working in Reynold's garden or ditchin' water into the Goodyear Hotel, my dad would put a few chinks of his own on Martin Walpole's stone. At the end of the week, the stone was laid in the back of a buggy and dad rode with his father to McLean. Together they set the little stone, stood back and admired it and drove back to Groton with the feeling of content that comes from doing a last good turn for a friend.

"Some Saturday afternoon next summer when you're not busy," my dad would always end the story, "we'll go over to McLean and see if we can't find that marker." Well, summer came, what there was of it, and with one thing and another, we let the Saturdays and Sundays slip by us. Dad passed it off with a wave of his hand. "We'll get over there yet and no great hurry," he'd say when we'd get talkin' old times in his room at night.

Last Saturday, you may remember, was as fine a day as we're likely to see before next summer. Dad won't stick his nose out of the house unless it's hot enough to prostrate most people with the heat. I had a leaky faucet to fix, a porch to paint and a blackboard full of chores to erase, but it suddenly came to me — maybe in the face of all that work — that this was the day to find Martin Walpole's headstone.

Dad had his hat in his hand before I'd finished tellin' him what was up. We drove out South Main Street, passed the old Carey homestead, across the bridge and by the McKane farm, around the corner and by the little house where Grandpa and Grandma Greenan used to live. We stopped once and watched a field harvester choppin' corn and dad marveled at the machine as any man might that's worked a day in the field with a corn knife.

We drove through McLean. As we crossed the tracks on the way to St. Patrick's Church, dad nudged me and pointed to the left side of the road. "Right there," he said, "was a little hotel where I had my first glass of wine." We both laughed for if a man never takes another or takes far, far too many, he's not likely to forget the wherefores of that first one.

We stopped a minute in front of the church and read from the sign that it was organized in 1844 and opened in 1851. That was a good many years before there was a Catholic Church in Groton and I've heard my mother tell that Dave Mead would walk from Genoa and Grandma Greenan would walk from West Groton to attend mass there. Think of that the next time you're singin' "Faith of Our Fathers." Dad looked on ahead trying to remember just where the cemetery was. We drove a few rods and saw on the left the monuments through the trees. I turned off the main road and parked in the drive. We hurried out of the car as if, after all these years, the stone of Martin Walpole wouldn't wait another minute. I pushed open the cemetery gate. Dad followed me through and we both looked around.

It was cool and dark and restful under the shade of the pine and spruce trees. This was no finely manicured, every-blade-of-grass-in-place-cemetery so much admired these days. It was an old burying ground, grass tall and tombstones awry. But it had the character and ruggedness appropriate to the hardy people that rested there.

I looked at the lettering on the first monument I came to. "Bridget and Michael Walpole," I said doubtfully because the names had almost faded out. "Matthew Walpole," my dad corrected me and I looked again and made out the "Matthew."

"A great uncle of yours is buried there," dad said and I felt that just finding that out made the whole trip worthwhile. I looked around that plot but my dad seemed certain that the stone wouldn't be there because Martin wasn't a blood relative of the Walpoles that are so numerous hereabouts. He walked on into the cemetery and I followed along reading off the names, as I came to them, "Kane, O'Byrne, McCarthy, McDermott, Conlon, Kelley, Keenan." The stone we were looking for didn't show up readily so I left dad standing in the center of the small crowned hill and walked down the west slope. I uncovered a few stones almost overgrown with myrtle, but I couldn't find another Walpole.

It was all of 65 years ago that Martin died and I thought that a small stone might easily have gotten covered up in that length of time or, worse yet, I feared that the engraving done quickly and without proper tools had been so shallow that it would have weathered away completely. I looked back and saw dad standing alone in the center of the cemetery. He appeared disturbed and uneasy as though he'd come on a fool's errand expecting to find after all these years something he'd dwelt on since he was a boy. I went back up to him and he said that there wasn't much point in looking further. But I told him to hold on a minute and went down the east slope. I was no more that halfway down when I saw it. I called, "Here it is!" and ran back up the hill to grab dad's arm because he had started toward me at a faster clip than his old legs would carry him.

We came down to the stone and looked at it closely. "Martin Walpole" was all that was on it. No date or sentiment was inscribed and unless you knew the story behind it you'd have passed it by without a second look. The lettering was rough but square except for the "N" which looked as though a small boy had tried his hand at the chisel and let it get away from him. The stone had been pushed askew by an enormous spruce tree which grew right out of Martin Walpole's grave. As I looked up to the top of the tree, I thought that any man would be proud to have that for a monument. But dad was all eyes for the stone and when you think of it, there was the Hand of God and the hand of man working together. And this day, as on the day so many years ago when Tom lugged the stone into the cemetery and set it on the fresh unmarked grave, Martin Walpole must have felt well remembered.

We stood a minute. Beyond the cemetery a team of horses hitched to a lumber wagon was being driven into the field. A pair of collie dogs, one ahead of the horses and the other behind the wagon, proudly escorted the rig. It was a sound and a sight, one of the few maybe in this mad age, that would have reassured the McCarthys, and the Keenans, and the Conlons and the Kelleys.

We turned to go and I sensed that great as his pleasure had been in finding the stone, dad had had an even greater pleasure in turning it over in his mind through the years, the very day he was living now. Like any man, he hated to see a good story come to an end. We reached the cemetery gate. He changed hands with his cane, looked back and shook his head.

"Curiosity," he said, "is a great thing until it's satisfied."

Gerald before his first haircut (1916)

School Days. When September comes, who doesn't daydream a little about going back to school? Do I hear groans from the younger set already hard at their homework?

Memories of my first day at school have been overshadowed by the momentous occasion that immediately preceded it. I was the childhood victim of the family tradition of waiting until one was five years old for the first hair cut. Although I had the male members of the family on my side, I never did get rid of shoulder length curls until the janitor practically had his hands on the rope to ring the bell for school to open.

My boyhood hero, and I still have a nice warm feeling for him, was the barber who gave me that first mass haircut — Joe Cartledge. Joe's shop was in the Groton Hotel then and the chair was set so the customer and Joe could look out the big window on the east side at anything that might happen on Cortland Street. Joe never had a happier or more cooperative customer in his chair. Nobody had to hold me in. The only time I got out of control was when my brother George came 'round the corner pulling the Red Star Bakery wagon full of bread for Gene Langdon's store. I almost jumped out of the chair to make sure that he'd see us men getting our own way at last.

Mrs. Johnson was my first grade teacher. She had managed five Barrys before me and she managed me and the class with the authority and sternness which was much admired then — especially in first grade teachers. There was no nonsense in Mrs. Johnson's room, but she couldn't very well prevent an occasional damp disaster nor the confusion which followed. Once in a while someone would get too interested in coloring, or be too shy to give the signal which we presume has remained unchanged through the years.

One rainy morning, my brother Johnny, who was in the fifth grade, deserted me at a critical moment, and I distressed Mrs. Johnson considerably by crying for no apparent reason. Because of the rain, I wore rubber boots to school. I had to change from boots to shoes in the hall and Johnny was supposed to stick around and tie my shoes for me. Because it was late he scooted off to his class room and left Mrs. Johnson to unravel the mystery of what was wrong with me. The beating that Mrs. Johnson believed in was not about the bush. She introduced me to her little back room, shook a little sense into my freshly cropped head and taught me how to tie a bow knot. I must have been a backward child.

When the going got rough in the more advanced grades, I was good at pretending I was sick. My mother was even better at detecting those too sudden recoveries after the last bell had rung. Oral topics — I wonder what they call them now — caused me to have a series of unexplained fevers, stomach upsets and mysterious maladies. These were cured by a behind-my-back conference between my mother and the sixth grade teacher, Mrs. Bishop. I enjoyed good health the rest of that year.

A few years later when Nelson Harris, a fine drummer with a complete outfit, left school, I was overjoyed. I took my five dollar snare drum to the first orchestra practice, set it up sideways on a chair confident that I could keep up with anything anybody had to offer. I could play "Stars and Stripes Forever" and "An Orange Grove in California" with the Victrola at home, couldn't I?

I've never forgotten the sad look on Mrs. Ryan's face when she saw me beaming behind the brasses. The only time I ever saw her any sadder was the day the State Music Supervisor dropped in unannounced at the school assembly and heard the orchestra rip through "Last Night on the Back Porch, I Loved Her Best Of All."

In high school, my chief concern was to find pants with wide enough bottoms. Twenty-one inch cuffs were de rigueur in those days and twenty-two inchers were downright snazzy. Sailor pants turned up two inches at the bottom and creased front to back instead of sideways were as close as anything I could ever find that looked like a John Held cartoon. Those big bottoms gave me, if no one else, the illusion that I had small feet.

Well, school's going to claim three-quarters of our family this year. Dave's started on his last year in high school. (This is something in the nature of a prediction which we'd like to come true.) Marg is sewing madly — and not too badly. Next week she expects to leave the corner of Lincoln and Barrows for Cornell. We hope they're able to do something there that we've never quite managed at home — supply her with an adequate amount of hot water. Marion has tackled Mrs. Johnson's old job of teaching kindergarten in the Dryden-Freeville School. We've asked her to be especially understanding to those fumble-fingered kids who haven't learned to tie their own shoe laces.

Thousands of cookies and hundreds of apple pies ago, I was a little boy. As happy and as self-centered and as troublesome as any little boy. I had toothaches and bellyaches, fevers and chills, skinned knees and bloody noses. I even had tantrums if I had to go by Laskaris' Ice Cream Parlor without stopping in.

There's a great deal to be said for a society which patiently allows so many spoiled little boys to grow up. Mothers, tigresses that they are, give society very little choice in the matter. A good many of us sons will get extravagantly sentimental on this and every Mother's Day out of gratitude for the protection from what might otherwise have been an early demise.

We all hurry to make up in a day what has accumulated over the years. But mothers have so much to give that we might well take one day for ourselves and let them have more of the other 364.

When you leave sentiment and even love out of it and coldly appraise motherhood as a job which takes so many hours of work — with no time-and-a-half for over-time —; when you think of all the little things like the number of times a mother goes up and down stairs or wipes noses or washes dishes; it all adds up to a staggering total. The more realistic you are, the more impressive it becomes. Motherhood doesn't need to be and shouldn't be viewed through rose colored glasses.

I can remember a good many days that weren't Mother's Day at our house. One rainy Saturday afternoon when I was ten I took a message for Father Crowley to Katie Lynch. It was a long walk and after I

John   Paul   George   Madalene   Gerald   Harold

Margaret McCormick Barry and John Barry

50th wedding anniversary in 1947

returned her answer to him, he gave me a quarter. I spent the quarter for a pack of Sunshine cigarettes and carelessly left them in the pocket of my raincoat.
When I came home, my mother was concerned because I had been out most of the afternoon in the cold spring rain.

   She hung the raincoat over the hot water boiler to dry and in the best feminine tradition felt in the pockets to clean them of all boyhood junk. When she found the Sunshine cigarettes and realized that I had spent Father Crowley's quarter almost sacrilegiously, she was a mightily disturbed woman. Unknown to her, I had already acquired a taste for Virginia cheroots as well as cigarettes but I never particularly relished the taste of either of them after that rainy Saturday afternoon.

And I remember her fierce, hurt look when she came into the kitchen unexpectedly and caught me stealing a nickel from the cupboard. I was on tiptoe reaching into the cup where the loose change was kept. She gripped my wrist and held me in that highly embarrassing position just long enough to burn a big lesson into my consciousness. After that it wasn't a matter of honesty being the best policy — honesty was the only policy.

But there are so many pleasant things to remember. When I was a child, what a comfort it was to crawl into her bed and cling to her arm. In sickness, disappointment, loneliness, that was my refuge. There was strength there and warmth and protection and solace. And there were days when I had little honors to bring home. There was a proper pride in my accomplishments and no disappointment that I might have done better. Or to be in her kitchen on baking day and peel off a steaming pan biscuit or dance a hot molasses cookie on my fingers until it was cool enough to eat . . . happy days.

There is one great test for a mother. She must have the courage to stand aside and let her child be himself — not perhaps what she'd like him to be or had ever hoped he'd be. A good mother wants neither the blind worship nor the subservience that is "momism." The ties to her son must not be bonds that he cannot escape. To me, this freedom to be myself is the great jewel in my mother's crown.

Maybe it would be more meaningful if I were a towering success and could say from some dizzy pinnacle of fame how much of what I am I owe to my mother. Because I am a very ordinary man, I owe her none the less. Perhaps this commonness makes any expression of mine the more universal. And greatness is a relative matter. In my life and within my experience, my mother is a great woman.

The mass of us struggle and wonder and try to express ourselves far from the center of the stage. Fortunately, mothers like mine are not unique, nor are my feelings toward her. Here is an honest, wholesome, universal emotion. At this particular time of year it is taken advantage of, commercialized and vitiated. But stripped of these inconsequentials, it remains one of the great motivating forces for good in men's lives.

I remember when Dates' Garage was being modernized back in the 1920s. The great event coincided with my acquiring a new hatchet. Hatchet in hand, I walked by the big plate glass windows and my eye caught the long, smooth stretch of newly painted wood sill. Completely unconscious of time, space or other people's property, I started to notch the sill with my hatchet. Every step I took I went chop, chop, chop.

John Dates stood inside the window and when he saw what I was doing to his magnificent new front he had something approaching apoplexy. He exploded out of the garage and every stormy, angry word he said was true. But there were the notches and there they stayed until the next modernization 30 years later removed them. It was just another of many, many times when I've been grateful for having a mother who believed that someday I would grow up.

When you lead your children gently toward the piano and attempt to fan the least spark of interest into what you hope will become a great musical flame, remember that where there is fire, there is also smoke — annoying, baffling, frustrating smoke. There probably isn't a parent alive whose heart hasn't quickened at the sight of chubby fists pounding meaninglessly on first the white and then the black keys. The vision of a musical prodigy swaying dramatically over the keyboard of a concert grand comes all too readily. It is one of the great American dreams — and one, unfortunately, that rarely comes true.

We modestly admit to some success in creating a lively musical interest in our children. It wasn't always easy. There were times when it seemed pointless both to them and to us. But we persevered. Our point is that having aroused a latent interest, we were not quite prepared for the quixotic turns it has taken, particularly in the male offspring of the family. Marg has been reasonably constant in her devotion to the piano. Oh, there were mild flirtations with percussion instruments and a brief, sad affair with a flute, but these were mere divertissements from the keyboard. Dave has been, and still is, a musical adventurer. He worked at both piano and drums, but he never really felt at home with music until the night he lugged home from school a big bass horn. Somehow, this surprised us because we had already assembled a sizable collection of fascinating instruments from which a musically inclined young man might have chosen. Dave "oompahed" religiously for several weeks, and we decided not only to play along with this whim, but to encourage it for our purposes. We pointed out that being able to play the bass viol in addition to the bass horn would have several financial, artistic, and social advantages. When Marion wasn't looking, we sidetracked a sizable chunk of the family treasury and advanced Dave enough money to buy a string bass. We have since established the wisdom of this purchase although it was rather seriously questioned — and rightly so — in family councils whenever "first-things-first" were on the agenda.

You might think that, having staked out a sizable area to the deep end of the musical register as his own, a young man would content himself to cultivate that area exclusively. But, once lighted, this interest may be, instead of a steady flame, a series of musical grass fires. After reaching a point at which people would pay him for playing the string bass — in our particular culture, not a very high point — Dave looked around and seized upon the most unlikely instrument — we use the term loosely — of all, the ukulele. We suggested that the guitar would be more worthwhile. We even went so far as to say that we wouldn't have a "uke" in the house, but Dave came back from his senior Washington trip with one he had picked up in a hock shop. We showed him how inaccurately the "uke" was fretted, pointed out the impossibility of ever doing anything worthwhile with such an inadequate contrivance, but he played it, though furtively, just the same.

Last year, at the end of summer school, we went to Schenectady to move Dave back to Groton. While we were packing, he took a deep breath and said, "Look,

Margaret and David and Nicky on a family hike to "North Ireland" train tracks, 1937.

No piano practice today!

you might as well face it. I bought myself another uke." With a determined gesture, he reached to the top of a wardrobe and brought down a sizable baritone ukulele. He played a few chords. This was a pleasant sounding instrument. We played a few chords and thought hopefully, "maybe he'll forget this when he goes back to school and leave it home for us." Although he forgot several other things, he managed to remember his latest musical passion when he headed toward Union again. During the year, he graduated with honors from an Arthur Godfrey Ukulele course with a standing which indicates a Dean's List potential for the inconsequential.

This brings us down to the immediate present and what looks like a turbulent future. Dave's current musical infatuation is the trombone. (He borrowed one from his high school teacher, Mr. Fisher.) A sudden move like this has immediate repercussions. Marion and Marg are planning a trip. Neighborhood real estate may plummet because this is going to be an intensive affair. Dave hopes to be playing in the band by VJ Day. In between glissandos, smears and sustained tones — we are left to contemplate that fateful day when we sat down together at the piano and we took one of Dave's tiny fingers in our hand and said, full of hope and ambition — and innocence — "this is middle C."

We have a temperamental doorbell. There have
been long stretches of time when we have had no
doorbell at all. There was a button to push on the
right of the front door but no electrical impulse was
transmitted to the dulcet tones of our chimes to alert
us to visitors on our threshold. Of course, this didn't
bother the habitues — they just pushed on in. But the
uninvited stood outside pressing a weary thumb and
boiling at the indifference being exhibited indoors.

This inhospitable situation was tolerated for several
weeks running and since there are only rare occasions
when we find it wise to use the doorbell ourselves, we
simply ignored the condition.

As such matters frequently do, the doorbell dilemma
came to a head at the dinner table — just as we were
about to descend on a fork full of cauliflower. We
knew from a variety of instinctive deductions that this
was something we had better not put off until
tomorrow, or next month. We had to fix that
undependable device once and for all.

We felt, however, that this wasn't so urgent that we
need cheat ourselves out of a five minute breather
after dessert. Dave, to our surprise, was all energy.
He pushed back from the table promptly and
announced, with what we passed off as boyish
confidence, that he would fix the doorbell.

We don't like to interfere unnecessarily with the
development of our children so we dipped into our book
of the moment while Dave puttered in the cellar. In
an abnormally short time, he rushed back up the cellar
stairs, yanked open the front door and pushed the

button. Bong! Bong! We got up to try it, knowing that if it worked for us it would work for anybody. We tried it twice. Bells both times!

It doesn't take much for a parent to over-estimate the power of his children. A moppet has only to walk up to a piano and come down hard with both fists on the keys and a parent thinks, "Chopin!" Fixing a doorbell is a modest accomplishment but we were intrigued with Dave's going right to the heart of the problem. This country needs — we began to think expansively — mechanics like that. Men who have an intuitive understanding of machinery. Men who . . . . . we broke off our daydreaming to ask Dave how he ever fixed that doorbell so quickly.

He hesitated a moment — a nice modest touch we thought — and said, "Well, I've been using the batteries to start my model airplane motor. I just put the batteries back and the doorbell worked."

Shades of Steinmetz! I could have done that myself.

♪

David graduated from Union College and worked in pesticide residue research. He received his MS from Penn State and worked as a biochemist for Norwich Pharmaceutical. He continues to play tuba in local concert bands. Tom (1966), Alden (1968), and Nathan (1970), are the children of Prudence B. and David Barry.

One day you've got a little girl parading grandly up and down the street. A lace curtain is draped over her head and she clutches your wife's first formal out of the way of a pair of wobbly high heel shoes.

So help me — you turn around twice and the girl who played "dress-up" is saying, "Dance with me, Pop, so I can try out my new high heel shoes. Got 'em for the Christmas Cotillion."

You look down. This is no make-believe. There's music on the radio. We whirl around the living room . . . Remember that session in the shoe store . . . Girl Scout shoes vs. loafers . . . lost that one in the third round . . . We spin into the hall. No wobbling. No turned ankles. The trial run is a success.

During the station break I settled into my favorite chair and the high heel shoes were piloted upstairs on an altitude test. They climbed at a steady rate, made the turn at the first landing without mishap and soared confidently out of sight.

I tried to read, but thoughts kept popping up . . . high heel shoes . . . college bulletins arriving in every mail . . . working papers to sign . . . lotta growing up going on around here . . .

I heard a confused clicking, a hearty giggle and Marg calling out — "Hey, Mom! How do you get down stairs in these things?"

Both of us went to help. When Marg tried to come down a step, she either caught her heel on the edge of the tread or kicked her foot out in a modified goose step.

"You'll just have to practice," was the only helpful suggestion her mother could make.

I went back to the radio, tuned in some soft music for reading and picked up my book again. Marg slipped out of her new shoes, eased into her loafers and scuffed off to the kitchen. I took a long look at those strange arched contrivances so dear to most women's hearts and opened the book to find my place. There it was . . . right at the beginning of a new chapter.

The new routine is in effect at our house now that Marion is teaching and Marg is in college. The change is as sweeping in our little domestic circle as the complete adoption of the Hoover report would be in political ones. Dave and I are junior partners in such endless endeavors as dish washing, dusting, vacuum cleaning, and washing clothes — and you know what, girls? — it's hard work. Once we get back in condition, we think we can take any of the above in stride. The big adjustment comes at noon when Dave and I operate a quick lunch concession for ourselves with a minimum amount of effort and a maximum amount of nourishment.

Oh! But it's different. I remember days when I'd push open the kitchen door and see an apple pie steaming on the counter and Arabian stew just being taken from the oven. Or maybe it would be hot Johnny cake and dried beef gravy with a tossed salad and Raisin Delight for the clincher. Why I'd hardly make it up from the table before the quarter of whistle blew. Great days — that's what they were and they lasted quite awhile, too.

Last week when Marion brought home the groceries, I noticed six packages of graham crackers. Graham crackers. Six packages. Those filling, but hardly thrilling, tidbits became to me a gray, unappetizing symbol of the future. All week, when I once might have been sinking an eager tooth into hermits or brownies, ginger creams or cinnamon dreams, I bravely munched on graham crackers. Even then, I hardly made a dent in the first box. I didn't notice — and didn't care too much — where Marion had stored the other five. This week when Marion completed her shopping, I noticed more of those familiar red boxes sticking out of the top of the bag.

"My Godfrey, Marion," I exploded, "you didn't buy more graham crackers, did you?"

"I have to get them every week," she enlightened me. "School snack, you know, for my kids in kindergarten."

Just to ease me over my graham cracker trauma, Marion baked a batch of ginger creams Sunday afternoon. Thus fortified, I'll lay odds that I last another week, anyway.

Marion and the Freeville Kindergarten Class 1963-1964

♪

Marion attended Cornell for a year and a half before her marriage. She was a homemaker until 1950 when The Freeville School hired her as a kindergarten teacher with the understanding that she obtain certification. She attended Cortland State evenings and summers until she received her Bachelor's Degree. She continued in the same manner for her Master's and then, Elementary Guidance Certification.

She was a nature lover, bird watcher, hiker, cross-country skier, gardener, seamstress, cook, baker, and traveler (Ireland, Greece, Italy, Russia, Turkey, Panama Canal plus trips and Elderhostels in various US states).

She received the Award for Excellence from the Tompkins County Foundation in 1987 for outstanding contributions to her community. Over the years, she was an active member of the School Board, the Child Development Center, the Health Center Board, the Housing Authority, Garden Club, Columbian Club, and Pool Association. She served on the Library Board after Gerald's death. Her determination helped build the addition to the library.

She died in an automobile accident caused by sun glare in 1991. It occurred on the same road and less than a mile from Gerald's accident.

Dear Marg,

One of the books that I read and reread during the summers that I spent as a boy on Grandpa McCormick's farm was *Letters From a Self-Made Man to His Son.* You have only to look at the kids driving around the campus in Cadillac convertibles while you're hotfooting it to Warren Hall to know that I profited very little from that bit of early reading. I just got in a hurry to raise up somebody to write letters to and forgot all about the success angle.

Since you've been a Cornellian for almost six weeks, I've had plenty of time to reflect on the 18 years we put in together under the same roof. You'll probably laugh at this, having had a close-up view of the actual performance, but before you were born I was certain I was going to be a model father. I fully expected that family relations experts would come to interview me on how I kept in such close contact with my children. As a precautionary measure, I subscribed to *Parents* magazine, but I read it with a certain amount of detachment because I felt by inclination and temperament that I was going to be a model father anyway. Probably every father-to-be vows that his family is going to be different. Now I look back on that early self-assurance as just the brashness of youth. There were so many answers I didn't know; so many problems I wasn't able to solve.

A modern parent lacks the authority that his parents had. Nowadays a father may tell his daughter that she can't go out of town after the Junior Prom but he decides it with all the misgivings that saying "No" brings. Something is gained if a dad does a little soul searching instead of handing down a quick and pontifical decision. But it's awfully hard to know when he comes up with the right answer.

The illusion of being a model father lasted a few years after you were born. I began to see that I didn't know all the answers when you were big enough to make a complicated ritual out of going to bed. I enjoyed giving you a bath, tucking you in, reading you a story and kissing you good night. But I found myself twinged with annoyance when I got to the bottom of the stairs to hear you call, "Daddy, I want another drink." Being a model father, of course, I got it for you. But I became amazed at how many things you could think of after I reached that bottom step. "You forgot to open my window, Daddy . . . You didn't kiss my doll goodnight . . . I'm too warm . . . Read me another story." There came a night when I abandoned momentarily my parental perfection and warmed your little bottom. This fall from grace, I assured myself, only proved that I was human after all. My venality was widened with the arrival of Dave. Like any man, I thought that bringing up a boy would be so easy . . . someone to take hunting, to play ball with. Boys, I discovered, are not easy to bring up. They resent your playing with their toys. They like to be left alone. They love your tools, your cellar, your attic, your living room — with you out of the way.

Well, there's no point in mourning over a lot of shortcomings and imperfections. There were days when there were no problems; when we all got up in the morning feeling silly and paraded up and down the hall or raced downstairs to let Nicky out of the cellar and chased him all over the house to see if a dog could figure out what happens when humans get a little giddy. Nicky, who had a higher IQ than any of us, used to play his part to the hilt.

And there were those few wonderful weeks when you and Dave thought that it was terrific fun to serve us Sunday morning breakfast in bed. The first morning you mixed up flour and water and stuck gobs of paste on cookie sheets. You were somewhat taken aback when they didn't pop out of the oven two minutes later as golden brown hermits. After a few more tries, you managed coffee, toast, bacon and eggs rather well. And just when you began to do the whole thing to perfection, you decided that getting us breakfast in bed wasn't fun anymore.

The most fortunate thing about our occasional family furors was when mother was after one or the other, or both of you, I could frequently stay calm and privately assure you that we weren't going to send you to reform school for being a half hour late for supper. When I got crosswise, Marion could always point out with some detachment that since you kids were unfortunate enough to have me for a father, I could hardly expect obedience, promptness, neatness or any other homely virtue from my progeny.

Sometimes at night when I set the table for dinner, I absentmindedly get out four plates instead of three. When I put your plate back in the cupboard I realize that we've come a long, long way. A long way since the mornings when you were three and Dave was two. We all had breakfast together then and just before I went to work I got smacked on the cheek as ardently as if I were on my way to Cape Town — and I dashed out of the house with enough oatmeal on my cheek to last me on that long a journey.

But these days are just as exciting and satisfying as any I have ever known. I can not remember what dreams I had on those summery afternoons when I put down *Letters From A Self-Made Man.* They were probably grand dreams. A boy can think up big things. But I'm happy to change them all for the chance to write a just plain father-to-daughter-in-college letter to you.

Love,

Dad

Margaret of the Cape Town Kiss, age 3

There are a few misadventures which might as well be recorded. Late this fall, before the big freeze set in, I noticed one noon an aluminum pan on the back steps. Being a little more conscious nowadays of household responsibilities, I brought the pan in. Next day, the same pan was on the back steps and it was partly filled with rain water. I emptied it and brought the pan in to be washed — it was Dave's turn to do the dishes that noon anyway. The pan was on the steps the next day and I wondered what in the devil Marion was leaving her pots out in the weather for. When she got home from Freeville that night, I found out. "I've been trying for three days," Marion told me, "to collect some rain water for my steam iron. Leave that pan alone."

You can get into an awful lot of trouble just trying to be helpful.

* * * * *

In my own backward way, I thought that the throw rugs needed a good, vigorous shaking. I like to hear them snap. It's a nice sound and it kind of lets the neighbors know that you believe in cleaning house. I took on this harmless chore with a lot of enthusiasm, shut my eyes as the dust flew, but had the satisfaction of hearing a real professional "crack" when I whipped the rugs in the morning breeze. After I brought them in from the back porch, Marion told me that rugs don't like to be treated that way. They much prefer the vacuum cleaner. This was advice I should have had before tackling a job on which I underestimated my capabilities. As I laid the scatter rugs back in place, I noticed that I'd snapped the end right off one of them.

* * * * *

In all fairness, I should report that Dave has made considerable progress in domestic science. Early in the fall I came home one noon and dimly made Dave out standing in the middle of blue smog. He was frying eggs and was so absorbed in the task that he was oblivious to the murky atmosphere around him. In preparing the bacon that preceded the eggs, Dave had fried it so fast and so long that the pieces had shriveled to the size of corn flakes.

But not long ago, he whipped up a cake, frosting and all, that sidetracked the graham crackers for a few days. I can tell from the way he's acting lately that he's thinking about tackling a pie next. He'll have a full measure of fatherly encouragement.

* * * * *

Earlier this week I was doing some thinking in my den upstairs. Life proceeded normally enough downstairs, but as I listened in, throughout the afternoon, I heard a recurring theme —

"Dave, you'd better look at the furnace."

"Have you emptied the washing machine yet, Dave?"

"Here are some things I need at the store, Dave. Better take these books back to the library too."

I started counting up on my fingers not only the number of things Dave does in the course of a day but also the number of months he's likely to be around the house to do them. There are a lot of the former and very few of the latter. Looks to me like there are:

Sonless Days Ahead

Who's going to shovel the walks
And hear my fatherly talks,
When Dave leaves home?

Who'll know where the axe is,
Think of my income taxes
When Dave leaves home?

I'll get "The Post" unmolested,
The last piece of pie uncontested,
When Dave leaves home.

There'll be no bike to bring out of the rain,
No high-water mark to wash down the drain,
When Dave leaves home.

But who'll run those last minute errands,
And waylay my wandering gerunds?
Who'll furnish the brawn
For our oversize lawn,
When Dave leaves home?

Not me! I'll hire a man
To keep everything spic and span
Yet, it won't be quite the same place,
Like a royal flush, minus the ace,
When Dave leaves home.

We're looking forward to our four-day Thanksgiving vacation. This gives us just the same amount of time off as school teachers and college students get — which is just about as good as anything we ever hope for. It would be all right with us if the 7 o'clock whistle blew Friday and Saturday morning so we could wake up luxuriously, roll over and go back to sleep again.

We're looking forward to roast duck and mince pie, to leisurely breakfasts, and getting the Christmas fruit cakes started — and most of all, to having Marg and Dave home.

Marion and I have been busy since September and the job of readjusting to a two member household came gradually and without too much difficulty. Marion is just beginning to remember to scale down the proportions of our favorite dishes so that the apple crisp which used to vanish in one meal doesn't hang around all week. Bananas have a way of not disappearing overnight any more and we were astonished to learn how long a two-quart package of ice cream lasted without Dave's undivided attention.

But there's something about the house that's different. I remember when the kids were little, they used to stay overnight at their grandmother's occasionally when we were going out on a Saturday celebration. It was always a strange and empty feeling to wake up the next morning and wonder for a minute what was wrong — and then you remembered, the kids weren't home.

If anything, these few months since college started have increased our appreciation of each other and tightened our family ties. Like most parents, we've enjoyed our kids at all the different stages from toddlers to teenagers, from Cub Scout to Cornellian — and we like the stage we've reached now. A couple of letters in the mailbox are as satisfying as an appearance in the kindergarten band or making the varsity cheerleading squad. There are compensations for having your family away — and the biggest one is the pleasure of welcoming them back. Anyone who wakes up Thanksgiving morning with his family under one roof has a lot to be thankful for.

Gerald, Marion, Margaret and David at 110 Barrows Street, 1950

Did you ever go to a friend's home where the colors, the furniture — where everything was just as it should be, and come home feeling as though you lived in a shack? Or go to a home where a couple is just starting out on a long, almost hopeless job of remodeling and return to your own castle feeling that maybe things aren't too bad? We blow hot and cold about our own house and our point of view is affected even by what we read.

Last week I glanced over Marion's shoulder and discovered she was starting an article in the August *Good Housekeeping* on the importance of accessories to heighten home decor. There were pictures of cute little gimmicks lifted from second hand stores for practically nothing ($30 is practically nothing) and planted artfully on an $800 escritoire. We finished the article together and looked up from the magazine at all the little corners, empty corners, that could be brought to life with tea caddies, toby jugs, bibelots, rococo ornaments and sconces. All at once we had that "camping out" feeling at 110 Barrows Street. Our house lacked the touch of a knowing hand that could pick up an old trumpet and make it into a lamp base, or unearth a porcelain head that had once been used by a phrenologist. Darn clever, these *Good Housekeeping* editors.

Of course some of our corners are not so barren. There's Dave's bass viol. What kind of an accessory is that? Maybe we could coax ivy to grow out of the "F" holes and dangle a brace of stuffed pheasants across the fingerboard. Another corner holds a vibraharp, a pipe-fitter's pipedream. This could be disguised as a roll-away bar but it is a challenge I would sooner fling at *Good Housekeeping* than tackle myself. Aside from these two well-filled niches, there are vast empty places that need bookcases and stands if we're going to have places to put things that we don't have yet but that we have to have for the "*Good Housekeeping* (August 1952) Look."

This feeling of wanting to fill the house up lasted about a week. To be exact, it lasted until last Sunday morning. After we skimmed through *The Times*, Marion said "Did you read about Noguchi's home? It's in the magazine section." I was stretched out on the davenport and ready for my Sunday afternoon nap — the first one. "Must've missed it," I said and passed out. Two hours later I woke up and found the magazine section on my chest and opened to the article about the home of Isamu Noguchi, the Japanese-American sculptor. Noguchi's home is a study in emptiness, in simple, uncluttered living. I looked up from the article and saw all the stuff we could throw away — and good riddance. Why bother to have the wing chair recovered and for more than the chair cost originally? Throw the thing away and buy a couple of cushions to replace it. Out with book cases, gimmicks, jee-jaws. Strip the house of nonessentials. It's the simple life, the uncluttered life. A bowl of beautifully arranged flowers in one corner, one picture, plain walls, the absolute minimum of furniture and you have a room that is furnished for the ages, a room that is classically simple, that invites contemplation, composure . . .

Oh, there's a jarring note.

"It's funny," Marion says, "that our September *Good Housekeeping*" hasn't come yet . . ."

Dear Dave,

I was going to try to talk to you when you were home but I never quite got around to it. Everything was so pleasant that I couldn't bring myself to do it. Besides, I feel that I write better than I talk so I've taken this way out. It's less embarrassing — and just better all the way around.

Every son, I suppose, takes for granted that his father is a lot of things a man cannot possibly be. Even if there are serious shortcomings, children have a way of looking beyond them — or of not seeing them in their own parents.

It hasn't always been easy for me to live up to my family responsibilities and I feel uncomfortable when I think that you may have exaggerated notions of the kind of man I am. I've thought a great deal about the effect of disillusioning you and I've been sorely tempted to let you live on in ignorance. But I can't do it. I just feel that it's better for you to know. You're certainly old enough now to begin to be realistic. Above all, I want you to go on being the same kind of person you are now. In fact I hope that this disclosure will make you even more careful and considerate than you've ever been in the past.

Well, I can't keep going on like a judge in a speaking contest. But I did want to prepare you a little bit for the blunt thing I have to tell you now.

David, while you were home, I used your Yardley's Aftershave lotion twice. And since you've gone back to school and left the bottle on the bathroom shelf, I've used it three times more. I don't know what you've ever done to deserve treatment like this but I just couldn't help myself . . . . . I just couldn't help myself.

Your abject, remorseful and depraved,

Father

Dave and Gerald at work in the kitchen, 1952.

We let our mind roam this past weekend over a wide range of topics of universal interest. We read and heard a lot about Stalin but we decided he wasn't fit company for Lew Beames, Henry Geisenhoff and Milo Morgan, the local men we've previously eulogized in this column. We also toyed with passing along some trenchant remarks from Phillip Wilkie's *A Rebel Yells*. All of this seemed a little unwieldy just before a Sunday afternoon nap — and even more so afterward. So we let our mind come to rest on a topic with which we've struggled first hand, which has wide human interest, and, with spring coming on, timeliness. It is wallpaper.

Some men and women exchange vows to love, honor and obey. Others water this down to love, honor and cherish. Nowhere in either contract is anything said about wallpaper . . . how to pick it out . . . how to put it on . . . how to live with it and not like it. A deplorable oversight. Many marriages made in heaven have a hard time holding together over a wallpaper book. Our own marital seismograph registered a serious quake the last time we attempted it.

We recommend that young couples, starting to slow down in front of jewelry stores, put their affection to the ultimate test. The size and setting of a diamond has never been an impossible hurdle. How much more realistic for them to stop in at a paint and paper store and start idling through a wallpaper sample book. They will learn more about each other's tastes and temperaments in a lively half hour session than any other premarital experience we can think of.

There are men, of course, who completely avoid the whole wallpaper issue. They simply relegate it to "women's work" and refuse to do anything more than pay the bills. We've always felt that this type of male harbored suppressed wallpaper fixations — probably from hearing his mother and father do battle over plain or patterned ceilings. This leaves him constitutionally unable to rationally choose between stripes or plaids, scenic or flowered designs. Such a man is shut off from a great area of human conflict and he is the poorer for it. Much of the confusion in the wallpaper business can be directly traced to these unfortunate males who have completely abandoned their wallpaper prerogatives.

Anyone who is familiar with our establishment at the corner of Lincoln and Barrows might be astonished to learn that, some time ago, we started with a calm, plain yellow wallpaper in mind for the living room. There seemed to be no such samples in any books we could find locally, in three cities, or two mail order houses. Marion and I started looking for substitutes and we kept getting farther from each other and from the plain, quiet yellow paper we originally had in mind. We've never admitted to each other who made the final choice. But I've never forgotten the noon hour I came home when the first strip was on. It was wild, orange and jungly. Marion's face was as close to an evil leer as I've ever seen it. The kids were torn between being highly amused and highly indignant. From somewhere, I summoned up the words with which an old painter friend met every emergency. "It always looks better when it's dry," he used to say. I said, "Oh, it'll look better when it dries," but I lacked the conviction the old painter could put into it.

Well, we've lived with that paper quite a while now. But not comfortably. We look up from a book, look in from the street, look at it the first thing in the morning or the last thing at night and try to recall just how we happened to get so far from our original intentions. We find ourselves wondering lately if there are any plain, quiet yellow papers on the market. Then we try to put it out of our mind. We're in no mood to live dangerously . . . yet awhile.

Marg in her high heels (p.64), Dave in his Yardley
Lavender (p.81), in front of the "plain, yellow
wallpaper," 1953

I'm inclined to think that any age is the dangerous age. Last year at just about this time was as dangerous — for a few minutes — as any I've ever lived. In my own peculiar way, I planned to make quite an occasion of Marion's 40th birthday. Big milestone in life . . .and all that. Well in advance, I decided what to give her and just how to present it. She needed, I felt, a good portable radio-record player for the kindergarten. Without her knowing it, I sneaked one into the house. On the night before her birthday, I waited until after she went to bed before getting out her present. Then I plugged it into the electric stove in an outlet that is connected to the automatic timer, set the timer for our usual getting-up-time, loaded the changer spindle with choice records, and went confidently off to bed with the happy realization that in the morning we'd wake up to the gentle strains of George Shearing's "I'll Remember April." Now I'd like to forget that April.

As always, I slept well . . . . . until Marion startled me into semi-consciousness by throwing back the covers and shouting, "WHAT'S THAT?" Profanity would have been justified. I had made a slight miscalculation in setting the timer so the serenade got underway two hours ahead of schedule. Minor detail. In trying to adjust the volume so we'd be able to hear the music upstairs, I had been extra generous. What was coming out of the loudspeaker was barely recognizable as music.

Just to foul the thing up completely, the arm of the record changer missed when the next record slipped into place, and the needle bumped along on the turntable and the edge of the record. It sounded like a couple of Greyhound buses were playing tag in the kitchen. I don't remember what I said, but it wasn't "Happy Birthday." Marion decided that a combination radio and record player wasn't just exactly what we needed anyway. Some time later she bought herself a new ironing board in which, I must admit, she has taken great pleasure. I face her 41st birthday now with the knowledge that I cannot possibly do worse. I sort of have in the back of my mind an idea that she would enjoy a power lawn mower. Now if I can just figure out some novel way to . . . . .

There have been a few casual inquiries as to whether or not I gave Marion a power mower for her birthday. Since I was mowing the lawn the other evening with a power machine, I feel that I should candidly admit that I borrowed it from my brother, Harold. At the same time, Art Adams, who is temporarily holed up just below us, was power mowing his lawn, and the neighborhood sounded as peaceful as a convention of outboard motor enthusiasts charging up and down Lake Como. For all its effectiveness, I found that a power mower is not a promoter of peaceful and pleasant thoughts. It is the outdoor counterpart of the vacuum cleaner — a thoroughly efficient device which I prefer to have used when I'm not around the house.

Having clarified to some extent what I did not give Marion for her birthday, I might as well go the rest of the way and let you in on what I did get her. The personal part of the gift was an inexpensive, but very colorful, fighting rooster — not the real thing. Marion's rooster is on a pin. This has a family and personal significance which I won't go into for the present. The rest of the gift was quite handsome in a crude sort of way. You see, I got an income tax refund check for $65 from the government. The check looked so good that I left it around the house for a few days. The next weekend when I could have used it, I couldn't find it. I didn't know how this new Republican administration would look upon such Democratic slovenliness so I decided to keep looking for awhile. No check.

Marion's birthday came on me rather quickly, and I gave her, out of the goodness of my heart, the check I'd lost for her to use as she wished — if she could find it. Eventually, I wrote to the Internal Revenue Department to make a discreet inquiry about people who lose checks. The very next weekend, Marg brought some kids home from Cornell. One of the girls was leafing through our books — Cornell men are so inattentive — and discovered the check in Will Cuppy's *The Decline and Fall of Practically Everybody*. Now that I've started government wheels inexorably turning, I don't dare to have the check cashed until I can assure the revenuers that I'm not trying to two-time them. It is quite possible that this check business will get all straightened out in time for Marion to cash it on her next birthday . . . . in which case I'll be two-timing her! Perhaps birthdays from now on had best be forgotten — a statement which I can issue with assurance that it will be heartily endorsed by both sides of the family.

I may be pushing things a bit but I'm going to announce here and now Marion's complete recovery from hepatitis. This includes her return to the workaday world of the kindergarten and the end of my noon hour idylls when I was able to come home to lunch as in the old days.

This pronouncement is made with the knowledge that I am a medical ignoramus. I have a full share of human frailties but one of them is not echoing, opposing or enlarging upon a physician's findings. I would miserably flunk the most elementary examination in biology. I can neither enlarge upon the functions of the liver nor calculate the conniptions of a capricious kidney. There is no virtue in this, except the facing of the fact that I am a medical moron — at least that.

However, it is hard not to form opinions about a disease you've lived uncomfortably close to for eight weeks. After observing one patient's gradual recovery, I concluded that complete freedom from the after-effects would probably not come until the end of a quiet, restful summer. That cautious prognostication was shattered late Sunday morning.

For all too short a time we had a visit with Mac Deller, his wife, Lou, and their three children. Susan, a composed and altogether charming seventh grader, Patty, a robust and outgoing younger sister, and Gregg, a handsome redhead, whose powers of observation exceed by several years his status as a first grader. While we compared notes with the Dellers on family and science matters — Mac once taught science in Groton and is now science teacher and administrative assistant at Dundee — Susan sat on the davenport and listened patiently. Gregg and Patty played quietly in the hall.

In a few minutes, the Dellers had to leave. At the door there was the briefest silence while everyone formulated a last pleasant thought before the parting. Into this void leaped Gregg. He looked quizzically at the two womenfolk of our family. Then with an uncanny sense of timing, he supplied what we'll call the psychosomatic push that hurried out whatever hepatistic hangover lurked in our household.

"I can't tell which one . . ." Gregg began. There was some confusion as everyone started talking at once so he started over again and louder. "I CAN'T TELL WHICH ONE," he said, "IS THE MOTHER!"

I don't maintain that the recovery was miraculous but there before all of us stood a transformed Marion, radiating good health, sparkle, buoyancy, joie de vivre, vibrancy, zip.

For the first time in eight weeks I was able to sit in the living room in good conscience and listen with satisfaction to the preparations for dinner. I walked away from the table and the dishes secure in the knowledge that my wife was once more equal to the domestic and professional duties that faced her.

Without apologizing for my medical miasma I say here that I know a cure when I see one. MARION IS BETTER. Marg is doing as well as can be expected.

Christmas is a time when a man thinks about his family, his friends, his job, the world he lives in. And even though it is the one season of the year to devote to others, Christmas is a time when a man also thinks about himself.

He tries to understand what his place is in this unbelievably complex world. A man knows a part of him that is very close; his mother and father have become one with the eternal quiet. He begins to understand what it means to be old. He is aware that his ties to life are as fragile as a Christmas tree ornament. He stands in the middle of the noise and turmoil and tension and longs for quiet and the chance to draw apart to come to terms with himself and the people he lives and works with.

Sometimes he does this by walking a few hundred yards to the top of the hill near his home. Sitting on a concrete well enclosure, he looks down into the valley where he has lived most of his life. He remembers now that some 20 years ago on a summer afternoon he watched from this same vantage point. His children, then seven and eight years old, came running out of the house to play train with their carts. After a few minutes, their mother came to the front porch and cautioned them about riding in the road. How clearly he saw then the part he had to play — every man's part — in the little world of his family. And he walked quickly down the hill and easily onto the stage of the drama of everyday life.

Now a man sits on the same well house on a clear winter's night and looks down on the Christmas lights.

How wonderful if it all really were a living Christmas card of innocence. How wonderful if all the worries, hates, sicknesses, misunderstandings and misfortunes could be drawn out like the core of a boil . . . and leave only peace.

Life is not changed by hilltop fancy. Man, strange and wonderful animal that he is, has learned to live with cancer as well as Christmas. He is still noble and durable enough to not yet be conquered by nature's or his own perversity.

There are enough problems if a man focuses his attention merely on his own home, his own street or his own town. If he lifts his eyes to the clear winter sky and sees beyond the valley into the far reaches of the universe, he feels how small he is in relation to the great sweep of life past, present and to come.

There is no bright star in the sky for him, no angels' choir, no one clear and certain sign. Finally the cold forces him off the well house and he starts down the hill to resume the play — an actor unsure of his lines. At the bottom of the hill he stops before a dark and deserted house. A deeper chill than winter's grips him. He looks beyond the bleakness to his lighted porch where an old trombone, burdened with ornaments, fruit and greens, hangs festively by the door. The universe, the valley, the town fade away and a man centers his thoughts on where in the world he most wants to be. A hundred steps take him there—and to Christmas.

If you asked me quick, "Who am I?"
I would say, "I am the grandfather of Kurt and Kris."
Of course, I am many other things,
a writer of sorts, a photographer of sorts,
a speaker of sorts.
I know a lot about typewriters
and the people who make them.
I know a lot too about the little town of Groton —
half mining camp, half revival meeting,
where the people are as lusty and lonely,
as terrible and lovable
as the people of any other crossroads in the world.

My wife is good to me.
She lets me wander down a hundred different roads
with no more complaints than a sensible woman
should make.
My son and daughter fulfill me with their goodness.

But if you asked me quick, "Who am I?"
I would say, "I am the grandfather of Kurt and Kris."
I see in them a little bit of my eternity.
And that kind of eternity looks good to me.

Grandpa and Kurt, 1963

Kris, Grandpa and Kurt, 1966

Kurt (1961) and Kris (1963) are the sons of Margaret B. and Arthur J. Schneider.

Groton

The Groton Central School building became the SCM building, then the Tompkins-Cortland County Community College.   It is now an apartment complex.

♪

"Groton was built at an awkward time" on the following page was written in 1960 when the town celebrated its centennial.

"Groton was built at an awkward time.
We grew into a community
When a man could knock together
A shoebox of a building
And stuff it with dollars —
If he worked hard enough himself,
And worked everyone else at least as hard.

We were not born beautiful, then.
And the transformation to any kind of beauty
Will be slow, painful.
But we should make it.
We should work at it
Much the way a homely girl can become,
If she enriches herself,
So lovely a woman
That her homeliness disappears.

Buildings reflect the people who live in them
And we should look for a happier, more honest
Reflection of the kind of people we are.
We should think about beauty
And act slowly but surely
To further advance
Not further scar,
The promise of this beautiful valley.

Groton beautiful?
A dream for our second hundred years."

96

There was a lamp lighter, John the Lighter he was called, well known even beyond his town, who loved to go about his work at dusk, trimming wicks, shining globes, setting lamps carefully to keep them burning through the night.

Passing from neighborhood to neighborhood, joking with children clustered around every lamp post, gossiping hurriedly with old women on front porches, telling men good naturedly what tomorrow's weather would be, he left behind him at every stopping place a glow of friendship that brightened men's hearts even as his carefully set lamps brightened the streets of the town.

A man likes to stand back from his work to see how he has done, especially a good man, a craftsman, a worker. John the Lighter was such a man. After he had finished his work and had come, by way of a steep path, to his own door, he would look back over the town seeing his blinking yellow lamps, his work; immeasurably proud of having brought light to his town, immeasurably happy for having friends at every light he could see.

Now, every man, whether he is a doctor or a factory worker, is a lamp lighter. To be a good one he must care for his lamps and care for his friends; he must trim a wick and tickle a child; polish a sooty globe, brighten a gloomy face. And after he has finished his work and has come, by way of a steep path, to death's door, he may look back, justly proud of the work he has done, of the friends he has made; justly proud, indeed, to have been a good lamp lighter.

♪

Dr. George Gilchrist became Groton's doctor in 1899. He was revered by the townspeople as not only as an excellent physician, but as a friend and counselor. He made house calls on horseback until he bought his first car.

In 1924 he diagnosed Gerald's rheumatic fever. He delivered both of Marion and Gerald's children. He quarantined Gerald with scarlet fever while Marion and baby David were in the hospital.

Dr. Gilchrist died in 1934 at age 58. Gerald's deep admiration for him prompted this tribute.

The tribute was read at Gerald's funeral in 1968. It was fitting for both men.

Every once in a while we get thinking back on The Vandals. If you're a newcomer to town, The Vandals will probably bring to mind rowdies tipping over tombstones and busting up playground equipment. Some of the natives will remember The Vandals with fondness, we hope, as a high school dance orchestra that perpetrated indignities — unintentionally — on such durable tunes as "Ain't She Sweet," "Dinah," and "Sweet Sue."

There were no "record dances" while The Vandals held sway in the late twenties. Louis Coleman was our most thoroughly trained musician. Lou played violin, made up his own obbligatos, and helped out with the head arrangements when the harmony was tricky — which wasn't very often in those good old, simple days. Stanley Moe played E flat alto sax. He had a fine ear and used to close his eyes and make up smooth sounding harmony parts. This saved a lot of orchestrating which none of us knew anything about anyway. Chuck Corwin was The Vandals' lead alto sax man. He played a fine strong horn and was most conscientious and serious about orchestra matters. Chuck's house and ours used to be back to back. Before The Vandals formed, we heard the damndest noise coming from his bedroom window in July. By August, the sound had taken on a definite musical quality. By September, Chuck was ready to play with the band.

⌐ The band selected the name to warn listeners that they might destroy good music.

Frank Ogden played piano. He had a natural, easy, light style. He could read and fake, and was good at adding those little touches and fill-ins that a small band needs.

The only brass section The Vandals ever had was René Born. René started to learn to play later than the rest of us and several weeks before he was ready we pressed him into service. The extent of his repertoire was "Sweethearts on Parade" and his trumpet sounded so good to us that we played "Sweethearts on Parade" every other number until Rene gradually broadened into one of the mainstays of the group.

Verne Teeter played banjo with us for awhile. In those days — and the cycle seems almost to have completed itself — a banjo sparked the whole orchestra. Verne played by ear and could cope with everything but tunes like "Russian Lullaby" which were in a minor key. Shortly after Verne joined the Vandals, we had an important job playing in the Corona Gym after a basketball game. During the week Verne was rooming at Bucky Langdon's on Main Street. Toward the end of the basketball game, Verne went to get his banjo and discovered it had been left in a room occupied by a recently married couple who had retired for the evening. A solemn conference was held and a unanimous decision reached that nobody had nerve enough to knock on the door and ask for the banjo. The Vandals didn't sparkle that night.

After Stan Moe left Groton to attend Bliss Electrical School in Washington, Don Curtice was hurried into the breach. Chuck Corwin took over the job of making up second parts and tutoring Don in transposing from sheet music to the key for his E flat alto horn. This tutoring was so thorough that for many months Don could transpose better than he could read a regular part.

We supplied The Vandals with percussion on a bass drum salvaged from a nickelodeon and a snare drum purchased from Wurlitzer on painful installments of $2.50 a month. We didn't know a quarter note from middle C and we were plenty blissful in our ignorance.

The school dances used to be held in what was then the eighth grade room — the long room directly under study hall. One season the Senior class became unappreciative of The Vandal's efforts so we jacked up our modest price in immediate retaliation. The matter was settled in Principal Frank Page's office — our first labor-management conference. Benefits weren't strictly cash, as we remembered, but we were promised — and received — special treatment with refreshments at intermission.

The Vandals played for occasional Masonic dances, at George Jr. Republic, and at the Y.M.C.A. in Cortland. When the social whirl came to a stop, the Vandals sponsored their own parties in the Odd Fellows Hall. Maybe a pleasant haze of memory has obscured reality but we recall those parties as something special in the way of young people having fun together.

Here is an exclusive interview with the rabid fox that terrorized Groton on Monday. When we reached the fox at his hideout he was resting from a hard day and at first wasn't inclined to talk. We finally flattered him into becoming reasonably voluble.

"Buster," he barked condescendingly, "I was feeling a little high Monday. I got no grudge against people generally, see, but I must a had one too many reefers and went berserk. It gets awful quiet up here on the hill and I got to cravin' a little excitement so I goes out and makes some. Not too bad either. J'see the headlines in *The Post Standard*? Made the radio and had the State Troopers tearin' around. Pretty good for one little fox, eh!"

"I had a high old time on, what'd ya call it, Dog Hill. I drove one lady frantic. She comes at me with a broom so I'm still pickin' straw outa my teeth. And kids — never saw so many in my life."

"I was easin' myself outa town after dark when I spied these three dames walkin' up Spring Street. Well, I says, guess I'll give the babes a whirl, so I nabs the center one in the ankle. Buster, that was the wrongest thing I ever done. The gal I bit musta been carryin' a fire siren with her. Never heard such screechin' in my life. And the other two pitched into me like I was nuthin' but a lowdown skunk."

"You know, I always wondered about women and them big pocketbooks they carry around. Now I know what for . . . to slug guys like me goofy. One of them gals must a been luggin' around a load of cartwheels just waitin' for a sap like me."

The fox moved his head cautiously in the best morning-after tradition and said, " I don't remember too much else . . . saw a lot of lights flashin' . . . heard the fire-trucks comin' and men shoutin' so I high-balled home." The fox settled back for what I assumed would be a fretful nap. The interview, plainly enough, was over, so I left quietly and started down the hill. I was some distance from his den when he hollered after me in a voice faintly resembling James Cagney in his public enemy roles.

"Hey, Buster," he snarled, "Is the Rod and Gun Club gonna have any more fox hunts this winter? Gets mighty uninteresting up here come January and March."

OBIT

This interview

Was scarcely through

When Reynard the Rabid

Was grabbed.

Foolish fox

Rest in pax.

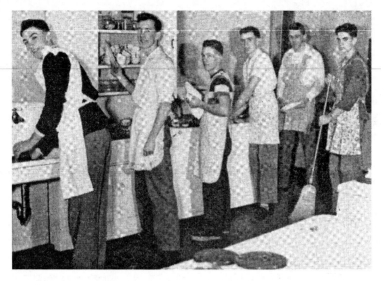

R. Hastings, R.Gallow, L. Todd, E. Walpole, P. True, D.Ryan

Most of my incoming mail calls for outgoing cash. Once in a while, sandwiched between generous layers of insurance and tax notices, coal, clothing, and telephone bills, I get a billet-doux. One came last week that give me a real lift.

Bachelors' Club
Groton High School

Dear Mr. Barry,

Seeing that you are married, we of the Bachelors' Club would like to invite you to a supper prepared by us and show you how we bachelors can do without the wife's touch.

The supper is to be Thursday the nineteenth at six o'clock; but if you would like to come a little early and see how well we prepare the meal, it will be all right. Come with an empty stomach because when you test our meal, we hope you'll ask for seconds.

Yours hopefully,

Ray Gallow, Secretary

I happened to be "batching it" myself for a few days last week, so I accepted the invitation. Did any bachelor, permanent or temporary, ever turn down a chance to eat out?

When I arrived at school Thursday evening, it was nearly 6 o'clock. Six bachelors were busily preparing an assortment of foods under the watchful eyes of Mrs. Carlon Tarbell, advisor to the club. Basketball practice had delayed preparations somewhat so I missed very few of the preliminaries. Dick Hastings and Ray Gallow were hovering uncertainly over an assortment of ingredients — flour, milk, and fat, which they eventually hoped to combine into pancake batter. (None of this Aunt Jemima stuff for the bachelors. They mix their own.) When the fat was somewhat timidly introduced to the rest of the liquid, it solidified into little lumps. "Looks like crushed pineapple," Dick observed. Ray just looked crushed. Mrs. Tarbell reassured the boys that they had made no fatal errors and urged them on to the final combining of wet and dry ingredients. "Just think — women have to do this every night," I heard one of them say as I moved on to the salad table where Palmer True was constructing, with a gourmet's fastidiousness, individual plates of fruit salad. Palmer's chief problem was time and Don Ryan was pressed into service to help him catch up. The meat cooks, Larry Todd and Eddie Walpole, had three frying pans of sausage sizzling. When men do get into the kitchen, they're lavish with the utensils.

Sniffing that sausage put me in the mood to eat. I was happy to see Mrs. Tarbell get into the act long enough to put on a pot of coffee and help Dick test the aluminum griddle for temperature. Both pancake cooks thought the batter seemed awfully thick and lumpy, but they were advised to see what happened. Dick scooped out a few measures of batter and turned them onto the griddle. The salads were almost completed. A platter of sausage went into the warming oven. Apple rings to garnish the meat were frying in sausage fat. The coffee perked and last minute table preparations were completed.

All of us gathered around what I assure you was a correctly set table. Eddie Walpole, president of the club, said grace and the meal started — a little uneasily at first. But as the pancakes were tried out and found not wanting, and the salads disappeared, and Larry Todd's wonderful sausage slipped rapidly off the platter, we realized that the first meal of the 1950 Bachelors' Club was going to be all right. Then we all loosened up. In the banter that followed, the cooks exchanged salvos of superlatives.

One thing had been kept from us before and throughout supper — what was dessert? After a hushed moment, the piece de resistance was brought on by its creators, Eddie Walpole and Don Ryan. It was a professional looking chocolate cake with coconut icing. A maraschino cherry graced the center. The cake was sliced into eight pieces and if it hadn't tasted as good as it looked, Bachelors' Club or no Bachelors' Club, I wouldn't have been able to eat it.

While we were enjoying the after-dinner amenities, Dick Hastings looked over at one of the stoves and said, "What's that water boiling for?" The Bachelors came out of their after dinner glow with a start when Mrs. Tarbell said they would probably need a little extra hot water for the dishes. The Dishes! Everybody waited for the assignments: Ray Gallow—dry, Dick Hastings — scrape dishes and help dry, Don Ryan — sweep floor, clear table and dry, Palmer True — clean cupboards and refrigerator, Larry Todd — chief drier. Eddie Walpole drew the big assignment. He had to wash.

After everyone was busy with their respective tasks, I had a chance to talk with Mrs. Tarbell about the Bachelors. The boys like to cook best of all, she said. They do a little sewing, and sometimes talk over family problems. Etiquette, and the niceties involved in phoning a girl for a date are covered in the meetings. Clothing, color combinations . . . . .

The room grew quiet as we talked, and when we looked around we found that the bachelors had deserted their respective posts. We looked in the gym and a girls' basketball game between the sophomores and the seniors had lured the boys away from their KP duties. They came back to the three greasy frying pans and crusty batter bowls. If any girls are worried about the significance of the name of the club to which these gentlemen belong, it is my considered opinion that there isn't a potential bachelor in the group.

In this week's Memory Lane from 1910 there is a little item that reads: "Monday, a nice boy came to the home of Mr. and Mrs. George Cummings. He is very welcome."

When you count up on your fingers, the answer comes out right, but it is a little startling to find that your boyhood friend made the front page of the Groton Journal 40 years ago. Bus Cummings and I lived next door to each other on Clark Street when this century was in its teens. With Bob Griffin, who lived across the street, we made up one of those tight little boyish alliances that precluded the thought of any one of us doing what the other couldn't.

The most dazzling contribution to the pleasure of our trio was made by Bus because his dad owned a Mitchell. We spent countless imaginative hours on the shiny leather seats going through adventures that would have terrified Tom Swift.

There must have been something heady in the aroma and atmosphere of a horse barn converted into a garage because I can still conjure up that new-old smell to this day.

Bob Griffin was a little older and stronger and quicker than Bus or me. Of all his accomplishments, the one I envied him most was his ability to spit between his teeth. I suppose spitting even then was considered a nasty habit but to me it was a purely beautiful thing the way Bob could sit on our topmost step and hit the sidewalk every time with precision and dispatch. Bus, as I remember, could make about half the distance and I, the secret of it eluding me completely, barely cleared my chin.

My contribution to this trio was twofold. I had a direct line to my mother's cookie jar and I had a brother who owned a billy goat. In those days of unhampered free enterprise, my brother, John, had collected enough Larkin soap wrappers to earn a cart with shafts to hitch the goat to. This was easily the second ranking attraction on Clark Street.

Gerald with his brother John's billy goat, 1915

Billy was a strong-minded creature though he was compliant enough when harnessed — if handled carefully. Once he was unhitched, he considered himself a free agent. With a half dozen boys always around, Billy was a frequent target for teasing. We all liked to see him rear on his hind legs, then hit the ground, lower his head and charge until his chain stopped him. One afternoon we were all playing this interminable game. Bus gave his attention to some side diversion and unintentionally came within striking range. Never one to miss an opportunity, Billy caught Bus squarely in the seat of the pants and bunted him down the steep bank onto the sidewalk.

A good many things have happened to Bus in these past forty years. I wonder if anything ever surprised him more than that attack from the rear when he was a kid on Clark Street.

Saturday night we filled in a last minute vacancy in Spiegle Willcox's Band. It was the first time in several years that we'd unlimbered the vibes for Spiegle and we had a lot of fun catching up on all that had happened since we stopped playing. We particularly enjoyed getting together with guitarist Chet Mead and bassist Harold Allen.

The job was at the Skaneateles Country Club. The starting hour for the dance was delayed because the buffet supper that preceded it ran overtime. While we were sitting around gassing, a handsome and gracious gentleman, who could have played Rhett Butler to perfection, invited the band into the bar to finish up the surplus hors d'oeuvres with assorted sandwiches and beverages thrown in. We rather enjoyed hearing musicians talk again. As we listened in on a half dozen different conversations, we discovered that through the years the number one topic is still women. Unfortunately, none of this happy talk bears repeating in a family paper. However, Spiegle told one story that's worth passing on.

Several years ago, the band was playing a job at the Auburn Country Club. Whoever put on the party had plenty of wherewithal. Caterers were imported from Rochester to rustle up some lush mush. Even the band shared in the frantic food. At intermission, the fellows sat around a table while waitresses brought in platters of lobster a la Newburg. The men eyed the upper-crustacean creations uneasily and waited for someone to give the signal to attack. Al Fisher, who was drumming for Spiegle then, brought the impasse to an abrupt end. He sized up the platters with the wholesome hunger of a hardworking musician and in his best W.C. Field's twang yelled, "PASS THE HASH!"

Spiegle Willcox Band

One of our most enduring interests has been music. Back in the days when the Opera House boasted an orchestra to accompany the film attractions, we went as much to hear and keep time with drummers Arthur Lape, Kenneth Kostenbader or Eddie Elian as we did to see William S. Hart add another notch to his six shooter.

One of the first orchestras we tried to promote consisted of Gerald MacPeak on piano, Bus Cummings on C melody sax and whom do you think on drums? We were in eighth or ninth grade then and the big wheels musically were Bradley Swartout's Maroon and White Collegians. Lee Coye played trombone; Elsie McMahon, piano; Lewis Jones and Ward Davidson, banjo-mandolins; Paul Hopkins, trumpet; Lee Hargraves, violin; Doc Tarbell, Hector Stewart and Brad, saxophones; and John Bradt, drums.

We just couldn't stand around waiting for the Maroon and White Collegians to graduate, so one afternoon, Bus and Mac and I went into the old eighth grade room where school dances used to be held and tried out our combination. It is a reflection on our musical taste that we butted our heads against a noxious musical creation of the moment called "O Katharina," and deservedly got nowhere. That trio died con brio.

Our chief musical inspiration in those days came from listening to records in the back of Kostenbader's store, hearing Coon-Saunders Nighthawks on the radio, and listening to Harold Leonard's orchestra, which came from Ithaca to play for the dances in the

Corona Gym and for parties in the American Legion Rooms (now the music room in the high school). Nothing sounded so good to us in that orchestra as the banjo, played if we remember correctly by Bugs Larkin. We borrowed an old five-string banjo from Kippy Blair (Mac had picked it up in Syracuse) and struggled with the intricacies of chords. We couldn't make much sense out of the banjo so we stuck to understandable, primitive drumming.

The Vandals, whom we've dealt with before, occupied us for several high school years. We had a brief fling with Al Stewart's Notre Dame Jugglers; tied on to George Fuller's lowering sails for a few months until all hands abandoned ship in the middle of the Depression.

From a musical standpoint, one of our richest associations came when Cortland temporarily ran out of drummers and Larry Harrington turned to us in desperation. Larry's big band was breaking up and small outfits were coming back into the picture. After a few years of seasoning, Wilbur Webster's piano, Don Kane's guitar and my drums backed up Larry's fine clarinet in what a good many musicians think was one of the best small jazz groups around these parts. We got our kicks from Benny Goodman's trio and quartet records, "Who" and "After You've Gone." I particularly remember an eight measure solo in "Deed I Do," which Goodman recorded when he was seventeen that really gave our quartet a lift.

One of our greatest pleasures has been to play for people to dance. Something unfortunate happened to popular music when people stopped dancing and crowded around the bandstands and eventually into chairs in auditoriums. A lot of pop music is highly listenable and ingratiating but we really prefer music that has so much punch and rhythm that people just naturally have to dance. We like the current Dixieland revival and those wonderful old two-beat marching tunes. But everything that comes out of the past isn't necessarily good. We heard "O Katharina" on the radio last week.

The Larry Harrington Band

It's surprising what 50 odd years will do for an unobtrusive item. What memories this one sentence brought back when we discovered it.

"June 15, 1899: The rooms on the second floor, in the Marsh block, in the rear of W.W. Hare's office, are being fitted up for a young physician, Dr. G.M. Gilchrist, who is to occupy them soon."

We are grateful that someone took the time to record Dr. Gilchrist's start in Groton. We can just remember that first office. It always seemed gloomy and scary. About the only cheerful thing in it was the doctor himself. We recall his giving my brother, Paul, shots for whooping cough.

We can still hear and see Paul squeal and squirm in mother's arms when the doctor got out the needle. We always thought he was going to stab us too but we escaped — and were grateful.

His next office on Church Street was more in keeping with his personality. We used to report to him hopefully before every baseball, basketball, and football season but he turned his thumbs firmly down on everything but baseball.

There was a sunny May day years later when he motioned to us from the corridor of the hospital and said, "Come in and see your baby girl." One of the sharpest and clearest memories we have is that first look at Margaret.

Do you remember the parade on Armistice Day in 1933? Dave chose to make his entrance that night. It was stormy and wintry, more like March than November. Because it had chains on, the doctor told us to take his Dodge Coupe. When we got to the hospital he called up and said to come back for him because he couldn't get his other car started. David, even then, was in no great hurry and the doctor made it with time to spare.

On a rainy, gloomy day near New Year's, he came to our house to say that Marion would need an operation. He looked at us and tried to break the tension by chuckling, "Can't somebody say something cheerful?" "Well, Doc," we gulped, "it's our wedding anniversary."

There weren't many times after that for him to come to see us. And there came the day when we had to go see him for the last time. We spent a good many hours trying to write something appropriate about his death. Our tribute to him, just as humble and inarticulate as the sentence devoted to his first coming to Groton, is recorded in the *Journal and Courier*, 1934.[*]

[*] see tribute on page 97

Today I heard that Milo Morgan died. A good many years ago when I was a kid on Lincoln Avenue, Milo was the man who lived across the street. He had a sharp, direct manner and I was more than a little afraid of him. But Milo had one accomplishment that fascinated me. I would have braved almost anything to hear him play the parlor organ and the mouth organ at the same time.

One summer evening I sat on our front porch trying to figure out how to play "Last Night on the Back Porch" on my sister's mandolin. I didn't notice Milo standing in his doorway listening to me. Suddenly he called out, "Come over here and bring that thing with you." I ran across the street eager and afraid at the same time.

As soon as I got in the house, his bluster and harshness vanished. When he talked about music he was patient and gentle. He showed me a little bit about fingering the mandolin. No trouble over notes. Just the pattern for my fingers to follow. We went over and over one of his favorite jigs until I could play it. Then he reached up on the organ and took down a little harness that slipped over his shoulders. It held a mouth organ directly in front of his lips. Then Milo sat down at the organ. His lips slid expertly up and down the little Hohner. His cheeks fluttered as he sucked and blew through the reeds. At the same time his feet were pumping up and down and his hands moved neatly in a strict rhythmical pattern over the keys to play a thundering accompaniment of chords. It all sounded very wonderful to me.

I worked and worked on that little tune until I could keep up with him. After we had raced through several choruses, Milo gave a little smile of approval, took off his mouth organ harness and shooed me back across the street.

I was on my front porch with the mandolin a good many nights after that and occasionally Milo would call me across the street to play with him. At the end of that summer, he moved away from Groton and I rarely saw him. When we did meet we talked over those summer evenings in his front parlor. The last time I saw him, Milo was crippled and shriveled. He was a man looking out from the shell of a fearfully wasted body. I talked about music and the old times but Milo looked at me piercingly and said, "By god, Gerald, you don't look too good." Well, it was my turn to be gentle and I laughed and said, "Now, Milo, there's nothing wrong with me that a good night's sleep won't cure." He limped off mumbling something about my not knowing enough to take care of myself and I walked away fully expecting to hear within a month that he was dead. But Milo lived for two years after that meeting. He had a lot of spirit and fire.

I don't suppose it's much to say but I think Milo would understand and be pleased to know how grateful I am after all these years that he was the man who once lived across the street from me.

Our neighbors, the Pouloses, have moved to Ithaca. Neither Main Street without Pete, nor Barrows Street without the Pouloses will look right to us for a long time. Pete and his family filled a fine warm spot in our town.

Pete with Eileen Rankin, Vern Metzgar, Bob Adams, and Red Carpenter, 1947. Note the trays of freshly made peanut brittle.

The sign out in front said "The Olympia" but everybody knew it was "Pete's Place." Its counterpart is in all the little towns across America — soda fountain, juke box, pin ball machines . . . deserted some nights and packed to the door on others . . . pimply-faced boys braving their first cigarette in public . . . ball games rehashed . . . wild plans made and abandoned. In Groton it was "The Place" for kids to go. A lot of trips ostensibly to the library were made with Pete's the ultimate destination in mind. The pay phone on the wall would ring and be answered sometimes for a casual inquiry about date bait and more than once it was irate parents tracking down an irresponsible youngster.

The tone of such a place could easily border on or be on the unsavory side. The place where kids congregate cannot be minimized in its effect on their lives. It can bolster or break down the influence of the home, church and school. Pete presided over his emporium with an easy, knowing hand. There was a fine understanding between him and the kids — and it wasn't merely "good business" on Pete's part. Of course he was an all-out sports fan and that gave him a big "in." His interests were young and his approach to the kids couldn't have been sounder if he'd had a suitcase full of child psychology theory.

We had a double view of Pete and Patty and their family because they lived just below us in what we'll probably always think of as the McGrail house. We can remember when we were a boy being taken to visit old Mrs. McGrail. We were usually given a cracker or a cookie but always with the understanding that we eat it outside. The Pouloses weren't eat-it-outside people. They enjoyed their home and shared it generously with others. Their children, Katherine, Nicky, Toula, and Johnny, who was blossoming into a real personality kid just as he left Barrows Street, brought to the McGrail house the kind of living that homes were built for. And "Cooky," their animated dustmop of a dog, reflected all the spirit and liveliness of a family that's full of beans.

We liked to see cars parked around our neighbor's house, the lights blazing and a party in full swing on Pete's "Name Day." And on summer evenings with the windows open we occasionally heard recordings of Greek songs and dance tunes. The warmest sight of all was to see Patty's mother, Mrs. Caroombas, sunning herself on the back lawn. After years of living on Main Street in the apartment over the store, we could sense her great pleasure at having a big green lawn and a long afternoon to sit in the sun.

We've visited Pete's and his brother Jim's new place in College Town in Ithaca and it looked most promising. Already, they have more business than they can comfortably handle. We wish them a great deal more than prosperity. We hope the Pouloses find in Ithaca a comparable place to the one they held in Groton . . . a position of respect and genuine affection for a fine family.

Back in the early '30's, Marion and I used to borrow
my brother Harold's Model A Ford coupe, preferably
when the tank was at least half full, and drive around
the country looking for "Our House." We finally found it
in elegant Cayuga Heights, a classically simple, white
brick, two story home. No dream was ever more remote.
We hadn't saved enough money to buy the key to the
front door of such an establishment.

We've thought a good many times about why we have
a home now. And of the man who advised us, watched
over us, and encouraged us over a period of years. He
was the late Henry Geisenhoff.

You may remember the office he had in the old
Chamber of Commerce rooms. He was usually there on
Saturday mornings. He would greet me on my way into
Tommy Holland's with a pair of shoes to be resoled. On
the way out he would look at me pleasantly through his
thick glasses, smile, and motion me toward his desk. It
wasn't hard to engage him in conversation, and once
joined, it wasn't easy to break off.

He started out by asking if I had ever thought about
buying a home. This inevitably led to his telling how he
started out himself by buying his first house, fixing it up
and selling it at a profit, then repeating the same process
on another. It took a few visits — and a few years —
before Henry brought us out of the *House Beautiful,
American Home* clouds.

He stopped me on the street one day and said, "Say, I
think I've got a place you and your wife would be
interested in." He came around later and picked us up;
drove us a little way out of town and stopped before what

looked to us little better than a shack. Henry was realistic though. "Now here," he said, "is a place you can afford. Maybe the place isn't too desirable, but fix the house up a little. Pay for it in a few years. Sell it and buy a better one."

Well, we were too proud, I guess, to live in a house we could afford, so we kept renting. But Henry wasn't through with us. The next week he climaxed a long period of indoctrination about The Savings and Loan Association by bringing us an application blank. "Just start putting away two dollars a week," he urged us. "More if you can afford it."

We began then to take stock of ourselves, our position, our income. The white brick house became a private joke between Marion and me. We still laugh when we drive by it on the way to Ithaca. It took us a long time to save $500. Henry preached his gospel to us regularly to keep us faithful to the cause. Because we needed more room, he began showing us houses again — houses we could afford, or almost afford. Marion began putting on even more pressure than Henry. When we learned that Sue Cummings Hill wanted to sell her house, we really got the fever . . . couldn't sleep nights . . . couldn't think of anything else for days. It looked like an enormous proposition then. This wasn't even an approximation of our dream house. There was an ugly radiator pipe in the kitchen right behind the sink. We had always thought that the front of the upstairs was a huge bedroom with four windows but it was divided off into two rooms. It was a well-built house, a better one than we could ever conceivably put up. We liked Barrows Street and . . . well, Marion was pretty insistent. Not our dream house, but over the years it has become our home, a comfortable, roomy, easy house to live in.

As we look back over the years of perseverance, of practical advice, of encouragement, we feel how much more Henry Geisenhoff had behind him than the chance to make a deal. He was a salesman, of course. But he was no Willy Loman, disillusioned at having peddled his life away. Henry came to see us occasionally and we made sure that he knew the day we finished, just as he planned we would, paying for the house.

There were a few people who regarded Henry as a sort of boulder in the path of community progress. We found him to be one of the clear sign posts in our life. He pointed and implemented the way for us and the important thing is that he must have for many others.

Henry Geisenhoff closed his books in 1950. We haven't been very prompt in writing our appreciation of him. But some things are better not hurried. We have a lifetime in which to be grateful.

110 Barrows Street after the "amputation of the South porch" (p. 157)

Some men stay awake nights for fear they'll miss Opportunity's knock.   Once in a great while, Opportunity will pound insistently on the front door and the man of the house will put on an old hat, pick up his rifle, and walk out the back door to go woodchuck hunting. Lew Beames was such a man.

Lew was an individual.   You couldn't run his characteristics through an IBM machine and come out with a stereotype. He had an attitude toward life that a man with a 25-year perfect attendance record could never understand. To say it negatively, there were a lot of things Lew just didn't care about. His friends were more anxious to see him recognized and rewarded than he ever was.   Who ever knew him without secretly estimating his financial possibilities? They were staggering. He was a master craftsman with wood who carried his talent around as lightly as some men pocket a lucky penny. If others could see dazzling possibilities in him, Lew could only see that a nose — at least his nose — was not meant for prolonged application to a grindstone. A fly cast on the waters on a cloudy spring afternoon might, or might not, return more than a mess of trout. Lesser men, huddled over balance sheets, tax forms, preparing to harvest the fruits of hypertension might well take a look at Lew's life and remember that there are several different kinds of totals to be taken besides those beginning with dollar signs.

Lew was generous in a simple, complete way that was incomprehensible to a small soul who measures out calculated favors. He could hand over six month's labor to someone he liked and let a cash job for the less-favored gather dust in the corner.

One of the most pleasant vacations we ever spent was two weeks in Lew's shop when he lived on South Main Street. Lew let us bring down an old cherry chest to refinish. He set us scraping off the layers of red paint. Earl Roloson, Lew's unofficial vice-president, showed us how to keep the scraper sharp. George Brooks contributed a piece of apple tree wood for the back and filled in Lew's somewhat sketchy directions. Except for the power machinery, the tempo and atmosphere were those of the Middle Ages and we've savored that experience all the years since. The now handsome chest is a reminder.

Lew built himself into beautiful pieces of furniture and in many places people are going to say, "Lew Beames made this" with the respect a jerry-built civilization owes to a craftsman. He had another rare and singular accomplishment. In this cautious, afraid-of-what-the-other-fellow's-thinking-world, Lew Beames was himself.

Each year the Activities Committee sponsors a banquet for retiring Smith-Corona employees. Although we have some responsibility for the program, what we enjoy most are the stories that come out at such a gathering.

Whitey Janorsky and Pete Stahl were major contributors. After Whitey told that Pete had been given the honor of delivering the first "Rose" typewriter, a predecessor of the "Corona" to Teddy Roosevelt, Pete got up to tell one of his pre-typewriter experiences in New York City.

He was a laundry delivery boy on a deluxe run which included the Astors, the Vanderbilts, and the Carnegies. When he picked up Andrew Carnegie's wash one week, the maid told him that one particular shirt had to be back at the mansion by 4:15 on Thursday because Mr. Carnegie was planning to wear it to a banquet.

When Pete arrived at the Carnegie mansion on that fateful Thursday, Andrew was pacing up and down the porch in trousers and undershirt. He had a fine head of steam up. Pete came running up onto the porch and the great Carnegie accosted him with,

"Young man, you're late!"

"Just two minutes, sir," Pete remonstrated. "It's only 17 minutes after 4."

"I know! I know!" shouted Carnegie, "but time is money to me. Why, every minute I make two thousand dollars."

"Gee, Mr. Carnegie, if you make that kind of money," the cocky little laundry boy said, "it seems to me you could afford to buy yourself a couple of more shirts."

A small town, like a strange man, takes some
   knowing.

To see a small town, ugly and plain as a stranger sees
   it, is not to see it at all.

There are doors here to be opened by people a man
   treasures beyond any reckoning.

There is work to be done that goads him out of sleep at
   night — concerts and play readings to be arranged
   for the library, music to be played, pictures to be
   taken, words to be written and spoken – too much
   time lost in the busyness of too short days and
   nights.

What can a man say about the town where he lives?

He can say that he likes it here and just possibly he
   thinks you might like it here too.

Life in a small town is dull, deadly dull, unless a man
   has the spirit to make it otherwise.

By lunchtime he can read a metropolitan newspaper.

By picking up the phone he can request a title from a
   library system that can get him almost any book in
   print.

By walking a block and a half he can drink beer at
   Don's or sit in on a discussion of the Cavalier poets.

By traveling an hour he can match concert for concert
   with his urban neighbor.

By turning off his TV set he can talk and if he is a
   particularly lucky man, someone will listen.

To put it plain, the most damning fact about a small town is that it is a small town.

Whether a man wants to get drunk or raise his voice in unrighteous anger, he can't keep it a secret even if he locks himself in his own cellar.

And if he contemplates an extra-curricular love affair, an all-night poker party or a secret meeting of one half — his half — of the Board of Deacons, he knows that he might as well give advance notice in the weekly paper.

Of course, it can be honestly said that the small town is not so small anymore.

If he chooses, a man can sit on his front porch and cool his hand and calm his spirit with a frosty Irish Mist and nod genially to his abstemious neighbor.

Teachers in small towns are freer spirits which has made them better human beings but not noticeably better teachers.

Even ministers have been unleashed from the severest puritanical strictures.

Cigar smoking is tolerated and some of the gentler vices — a can of beer on a steamy hot summer afternoon — condoned.

The truth is that a man can make a damn fool of himself anywhere.

He just can't do it anonymously in a small town.

Could this be — a man asks himself who often flirts with that possibility — perhaps a good thing?

What can a man say about the town where he lives?

He can say there is no gloss on it for him.

He knows it too well to talk about it like a real estate agent or shine it up like the secretary of a chamber of commerce.

A man just doesn't think of his town as something to be sold.

Sometimes he's too involved to notice that the church carpet is dowdy or that his own back steps need fixing.

If he listens, his pastor will call him on the carpet and his wife will confront him on the steps.

In a small town a man may get narrowed to a small group of people or worse, to a scrawny group of ideas, or to no ideas at all.

If he looked and listened and recorded what he observed, he could set down pretty much the whole catalogue of human depravity.

But in his observations he would also find much quiet goodness.

What can a man say of the town where he lives?

He can say that place is not important.

Happiness and unhappiness are within him and the way he looks at the world.

But a man has to live someplace and it is good for him
   to love that place — not blind to its faults; not blind
   to its virtues.

But to love it all the same as men through all ages
   have simply loved the town they call home.

We have added a new holiday to our family calendar — Peter's Day — in honor of Peter Kurosawa's arrival at our home. We celebrated recently the first anniversary of his visit with a quiet family dinner and reminiscences of a wonderful young man who brightened all our lives.

Peter is back in Tokyo now after spending a year in Syracuse and Groton as a Smith-Corona "Exchange Student." Of all his memorable experiences in the United States and around the world, we know that Peter will never forget the first weekend he spent in Groton. As originally planned, Peter was to arrive in time to see the Cornell-Harvard football game with us. At the last minute we learned that he was having difficulty with the second hand car he had just acquired and would come to Groton after the game.

Peter arrived at about six o'clock in the evening. We had a few quiet minutes of getting acquainted. Dave helped Peter unload his car. Then one of those strange weekends developed. Friends we hadn't seen in months started dropping in. By Sunday morning breakfast, we had 17 — all of us trying to pretend to ourselves and to Peter that this was the way things always were. Much later, Peter told Marion he hadn't been able to figure out "Whose was who."

We've often thought that if Peter's trunk hadn't been carried upstairs and stowed in his corner room that he might have withdrawn gracefully to a motel in Cortland and never experienced life in small town America.

We established a morning routine quickly. Breakfast started at 7:30 very nearly to the minute. On that first Monday morning when Peter pulled out Marion's chair for her to sit down, I felt like an unmannerly clod. In the afternoon when she came home from school, Peter raced out of the house to open the garage doors for her. I realized then that I was an absolute lout. But we had some wonderful times ahead of us and we knew this from the very first day that Peter came to live with us.

Best of all were the evenings after dinner when we would talk at the table — sometimes for an hour — about Peter's family, music, America, Japan, food, and very, very rarely, business. Peter was a conversationalist but not a controversialist. Whenever Marion and I ended up with opposite views in a political discussion and Marion turned to Peter for support, Peter would anticipate the tactic by saying, "Mrs. Barry, please don't ask me that!"

In the kitchen, Peter was a master. He had been trained in both Japanese and French cuisine. He cooked with grace and skill; in fact, Peter did an unbelievable number of things with grace and skill. He introduced us to Japanese cooking by preparing a soup made from seaweed, dried fish, finely chopped onions and carrots. The soup was a clear, delicate color. We were prepared for an adventurous and somewhat exotic taste but both of us found Peter's soup to be simply delicious. In fact, every dish he cooked, from suki-yaki to broiled chicken to a thick chicken soup, we liked and ate with relish. With a little cold boiled rice, soy sauce, saki, onions, celery and any leftover in the refrigerator, Peter could improvise an appetizing dish. This had a permanent effect on Marion's cooking and I find that leftovers Japanese style are more palatable than leftovers American style . . . even with Peter gone.

We still have Peter's chopsticks in the kitchen — one of many mementoes large and small to remind us that he lived here for nine months. He was a master bacon fryer and always used the chopsticks to meticulously turn the strips. Marion now uses them to fry the bacon also. I find them wonderful for making martinis — although I haven't yet mastered the technique of getting the olives out of the bottle. I use them often in an effort to offset the deleterious effect that hot fat may have on the wood. We want to keep Peter's chopsticks a long, long time.

Some time after Peter came to Groton we learned that his adventures that first weekend were not confined to the corner of Lincoln Avenue and Barrows Street. On his way to Groton from Syracuse, he drove very slowly. He was unsure of his car and even more unsure of his ability to drive consistently on the right side of the road. The Japanese follow the English custom — a point of lively debate between Marion and Peter — and drive on the left. Peter drove so slowly that a State Trooper stopped him for obstructing traffic. There is no more eloquent testimony to Peter's charm than the fact that the trooper forgot about the charge and treated him to a reassuring cup of coffee in the Marybelle Diner.

A few days later Peter drove to Syracuse and back. Just outside Cortland on his return trip he picked up a "hitch-hike boy." The boy told Peter he was going to Groton City. When they approached the turn on the Cortland-Groton road where Peter could have either let the boy off or taken him to Groton City, he assured the boy that he knew where Groton City was and drove him right to the main intersection in Groton.

"This, Groton City," Peter said. (And Peter had his own special pronunciation of Groton . . . something between Grawton and Growton, with the accent on the last syllable.)

"No," the boy told him somewhat desperately, "Groton City is back there."

Peter looked again for the familiar landmarks, the bank, the hotel, and said very positively, "THIS GROWTON CITY."

Peter was finally convinced that there was a separate Groton City and he was so anxious to see what kind of a metropolis this might be that he turned around and drove the boy to his home.

The hamlet fascinated Peter. Later he went to church suppers there and I think that Groton City, the name and the place, clearly represented to him the paradox that is America.[♪]

Peter's last day with us started very early in the morning. We were awakened by the fire whistle. We looked out the bedroom window and saw the flames shooting from McMahon's Garage a block from our home.

We called Peter. He took one look, said, "Oh!" and disappeared into the morning with his camera.

In the hours that followed we had to revise Peter's schedule. Instead of leaving at eleven in the morning for Syracuse, we finished our work at the plant in the early afternoon. We took Peter to his second American clambake, sponsored by the Activities Committee, where he enjoyed the food and the kite flying contest.

When we finally left Groton in the late afternoon, Peter asked — and he rarely made a direct request — if we might drive through Groton City on the way. We stopped on the east side of the valley at a point he decided was perfect for taking pictures of an unforgettable hamlet.

We didn't say good-bye at the University Club in Syracuse because we had learned from Peter that good-byes are not said. We talked about how soon we

[♪] the population of GROTON CITY is 37

would see one another again. And these were not idle promises. We drove away gaily waving to one of the warmest and finest human beings we know.

Many months later, Marion and I were driving home from Cortland. The car radio was tuned to an international exchange program of the Canadian Broadcasting Company. One segment was a broadcast of a children's chorus from Japan. When those peculiarly clear voices started to sing a song that was familiar to us because of a recording Peter had given us, we were grateful that it was after dark and we could hide a little bit from each other the fact that saying "not good-bye" to Peter was much more difficult than we had pretended.

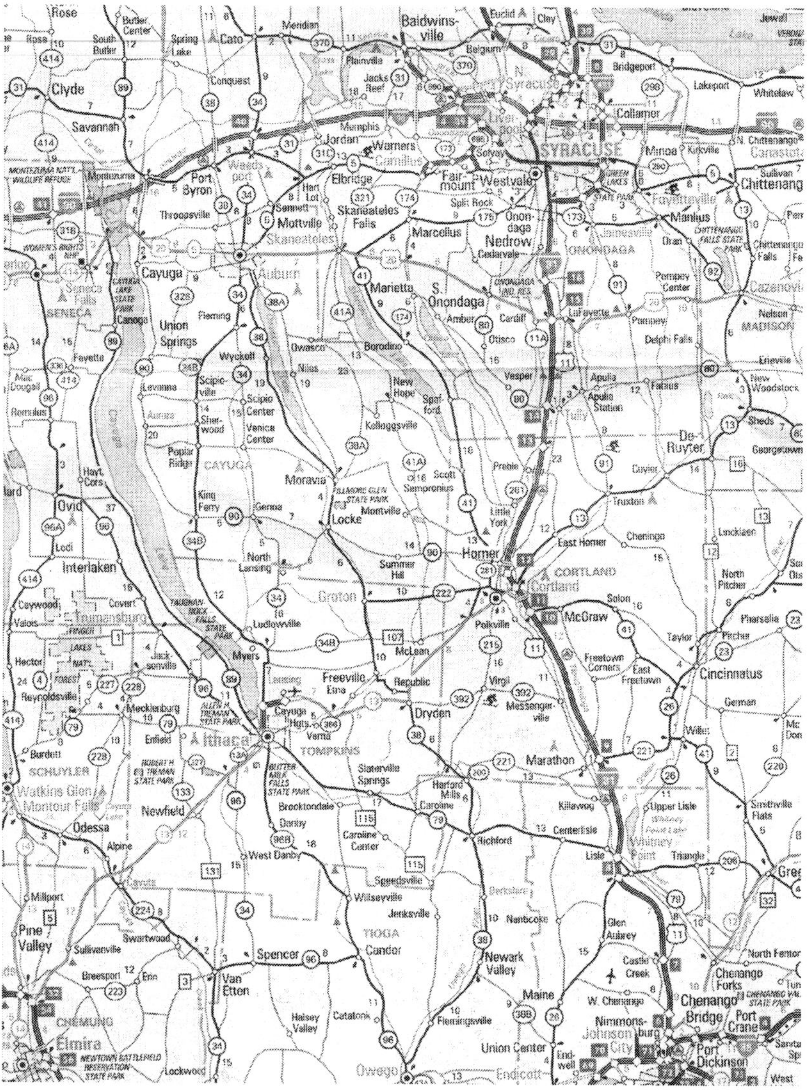
Baldwinsville
Clyde
Savannah
Port Byron
Jordan
Elbridge
Skaneateles
Auburn
SYRACUSE
Westvale
Manlius
Chittenango
Cayuga
Seneca Falls
Union Springs
Marietta
Onondaga
Moravia
Locke
Genoa
Ovid
Interlaken
Trumansburg
Groton
Homer
Cortland
McGraw
Dryden
Freeville
Ithaca
Cayuga Hgts.
Newfield
Watkins Glen
Odessa
Spencer
Van Etten
Candor
Newark Valley
Owego
Elmira
Marathon
Cincinnatus
De Ruyter
Whitney Point
Lisle
Chenango Bridge
Port Dickinson
Union Center
TOMPKINS
SCHUYLER
CAYUGA
TIOGA
CHEMUNG
ONONDAGA
CORTLAND
SENECA
MADISON

The answer to this question is simple only to the people who live or work there. During the Ithaca registration for classes at the evening division of the Tompkins-Cortland Community College, President Hushing Bahar recommended to an Ithacan who lacked her certificate of residency that she register the following night in Groton.

Back came the age old response.

"Where is Groton?"

Another — more of a world traveler-type who couldn't admit to complete ignorance of anything — responded to the president's invitation by saying, "Groton? I've heard of it but I've never been there."

Possibly.

She was really thinking of that famous Boys' School, or the submarine base or Croton-on-the-Hudson, a favorite repository for Groton's mail in pre-zip code days.

But sending a letter to Groton is quite another thing.

It's the getting there that counts. It is not quite enough to say that Groton is in northeastern Tompkins County — especially in such an inner-directed community as Ithaca.

One fairly new resident — a rare breed — has figured out a quick way to tell his Ithaca friends — none of whom ever heard of Groton — how to get there.

"You go up new Route 13, see," he says confidently — "turn left at Howard Johnson's — drive about three miles until you come to a stop sign — turn right and drive six more miles until you come to another stop sign — turn left and drive three more miles and you'll come to Groton."

This sounds terribly clear and accurate to someone who has lived in Groton a lifetime.

Nearly all Ithacans react to the instructions politely even though they know in their hearts the Stop sign business is meaningless. There really is no Groton at the end of the left and right and left turnings.

A few people have arrived in Groton over the years. Some accidentally. A rare few intentionally.

When a visitor breaks the barrier nowadays, he will hardly have time to congratulate himself on the achievement before a native will tell him in one breath that he is now in a community with the third lowest electric rate in New York State plus a brand new sewer system with a zooming downdraft plus a water supply adequate for more people than will ever make their way inside the corporate limits.

Breath number two will take in the Groton Rod and Gun Club which has two members of international renown who somehow made their way out into the world and back without ever getting lost and the swimming pool which is ten years old but seems like yesterday and two lovely schools and . . . and . . . and . . . the most recent topper was the recreation center with 18 hole golf course, swimming pool and tennis courts until the Tompkins-Cortland Community College located itself right on Main Street. In Groton.

Somehow or other, people are going to have to find their way to Groton.

The problem is historical. In the early days, an embarrassing letter arrived in the local Post Office. The address read:

```
Remington Typewriter Co.
Main Street
Groton, New York
```

The letter is buried deep in the old Corona archives. Equally embarrassing was a letter addressed:

```
The Corona Typewriter Co.
145 West 32nd Street
Groton, New York
```

This is the only time in its history that Groton was confused with a great metropolitan center. But a town needs a few moments like this to sustain itself under the eternally abrasive questioning.

"Where is Groton?"

Groton is a little over one hundred years old. It was not born beautiful. Too many shoebox buildings and a disposition toward practicality and manufactory to ever take quite enough time to pretty up the place.

Steps are being taken. You will notice, if you ever make the journey — left at Howard Johnson's etc. — that attractive signs inform you that you have indeed arrived.

"The least a community could do," you'll say, "after my taking the trouble to get here."

If the natives are too garrulous, you can stop them at any point during the electric rate/sewage system harangue by asking,

"Now where could I get a bite to eat?"

That's a harder question to answer than how to get to Groton in the first place.

A man who did not have to find Groton because he was born there and never got out because he wasn't sure he could find his way back to some lovely people, thinks that some day there will be a good answer to the question.

But don't stay away.

Drive out new Route 13.   Turn left at Howard Johnson's.   Turn   right   at   the   next   stop signandleftatthenextstopsignandyou'llsoonbeinGroton.

But don't forget to bring your lunch.

Groton Band in front of Smith-Corona-Marchant, 1965

Other

"We stand here reverent but unknowing,

      willing but unable to believe.

We have no hope for eternal life

      and no fear of eternal damnation.

We see our importance and unimportance

      in an ordered universe.

We hold ourselves responsible

      for neighbor and self.

We ask for strength

      to face life with courage.

We hope to pass on the heritage

      we have received from others.

We know good and evil,

      love and hate,

      life and death,

      and partly understand them.

We take this moment of living to ask,

      can a man know more?"

Marion and Gerald, 1961

Almost every magazine these days has a section devoted to making marriage work. After being analyzed in print by four or five marital relations experts, you get the feeling that maybe the law of averages is working against you and you begin to wonder how much longer the old homestead will hang together.

After a quick run over the latest and grimmest set of divorce figures, these questionnaires usually hit you where your Armour is weakest:

"Are you a good husband?"

"Do you look forward to each new day?"

"Are you free from any financial strains?"

You're supposed to keep score on 20-odd questions such as these and an honest man will have to cheat considerably to get a barely passing mark.

After several years of sparring in the connubial ring, we've scored no knockdowns but the in-fighting has been plenty lively. We sort of hope that the match will end in a draw, but these questionnaires have us worried. The woman who was mad about you yesterday may be just plain mad at you today.

All of us have an exaggerated idea of what to expect from marriage — and from life. After being nurtured on the success formula, a lot of us have to learn to live on a level considerably below the social and material ionosphere. Contentment isn't the big part of the American dream. We're where we are because a lot of people pushed — pushed west, pushed up, pushed down. Yes, there's even been some pushing around. Whether you're a pusher or one of the pushed, aren't there times it all seems slightly frantic? We don't long for a return to the horse and buggy days or the thirteenth century. We do feel that the national cruising speed could be lowered a notch with benefit to all hands — and all marriages.

A man needs to have signs and portents. He needs to get his bearings. There are mighty few things anyone can be sure of these days. We've devised our own little test of marriage solidarity, but we wouldn't suggest lighting out for Reno if it shouldn't work for you. But if it does work, mister, you've got the real thing.

La Pomme D'Amour For Sure

The petals that a daisy's got
Won't tell who loves or loves you not.
That answer's as elusive
As mercury in a new sieve.
I know one sure measure
To test the one you treasure —
Eat an apple,
The fruit which brought us all such pains,
And sit uneasily dangling the remains.

If she will leave her book to take the core,
Rejoice, no one could ever love you more.

This week, "Reflections" has a birthday — the column is one year old. As we hitch up our diapers and take a furtive look over our shoulder, we're conscious of not having traveled very far. At least, we've taken that first big step, and frankly, we're somewhat surprised to still be on our feet. End of round one.

Writing "Reflections" has been good for us. We want to thank all of you who've been kind enough to tell us that you look for the column each week. We hate to admit it, but we got the most comment when we didn't write anything at all. Being no stickler for unbroken records, we've had to answer, "What happened to the column this week?" a half dozen times.

Some of our best work was done in desperation to keep that number from being any higher. "The Rabid Fox Interview" was dashed off one Monday noon hour. That story made the Radio Edition of the Weekly Press and was submitted by WHCU, along with the rest of the half hour broadcast, to two radio contests. We kept the piece about Grandfather McCormick "never doing the like in a man's house yet" in a folder for several months. One uninspired Sunday evening, we decided to risk the wrath of our formidable Aunt Ann and use it. That was one of "Reflections" most successful weeks.

Our most ambitious column came at Christmas but we've learned that Christmas is not a time to get expansive. The only thing people read in December is shopping lists.

It's a good feeling to have written about "The Vandals," "Marg's High Heel Shoes," and to have heard Jack Deal at WHCU read, "When Dave Leaves Home." No deathless prose. No jeweled verse. Just a good honest try to get down from week to week some of the things we've thought about.

Well, we've sucked in a lot of air just to blow out one little candle. If you think that the gust rattling your shutters and ripping off your storm door is March wind, you're mistaken. That's just us, "Reflections." Our first birthday — "POOF" — was a happy one.

My Grandfather McCormick was a devout Irishman
not above thinking that a walk through his orchard by
the nuns was pleasing to God and an act of
propitiation that bore fruit. And he'd point out to you
in the fall the enormous Kings and the thrifty Spies, if
the nuns had walked in his orchard in the spring. As
does any man of any faith, my Grandfather liked to be
on close terms with his pastor and a call by the clergy
to the McCormick farm involved enormous helpings of
ham and Irish history — Grandpa served both with a
lavish hand.

One of the last pastors who ministered to him was a
young, virile, trumpet-voiced priest, Father Frederick
Staub. When he sang, "Gloria in Excelsis Deo," at
High Mass, the roof of St. Bernard's Church in Scipio
fluttered heavenward. But Father Staub's veneration
equaled his volume. God had little choice but to listen
to the praise that ascended from that country church.

The young priest was a popular man which, of
course, heightened his stature as a potential listener
to my Grandfather's discourse on Plunkett's place in
Irish history. But the priest was hard to pin down to a
leisurely afternoon under the pine trees on the
McCormick front lawn. He was a vital man, a doer,
and he set fire to more than one smouldering Christian
in his calls throughout the parish. And when at last
he got an automobile, Father Staub was able to spread
the Word of God and the dust of Scipio roads in even
greater profusion.

One summer morning, after the dew had gone off the grass, my Grandfather took his scythe and started to mow the roadside on his fields that faced the road to Cascade. It was a task he took great pride in and he mowed and muttered grand thoughts to himself, forming the fine phrases he'd toss off to the next unwary listener he could corner into hearing him out.

The morning quiet was broken by the unfamiliar hum of an automobile. The old man looked back toward the house and he could see, coming over the small knoll, a Dodge touring car that was driven at a speed that presumed not only the providence of a beneficent divinity but the assistance of a battalion of guardian angels. My grandfather's eyes, that some days couldn't see the teapot on the other end of the table and on other days could catch the daring hemline of one of his granddaughter's dresses, glimpsed the frantically waving arm and the clerical collar of Father Staub. Maddened by the devilish machine which could propel a man out of earshot in a second, choked by the dust and the many things he had to say in the short time he had to say to them, Grandpa flung his scythe at the column of dust rising halfway now to Cascade and roared, "God bless the days when we had time to stop and pass the time of day with one another!"

After you've been out bowling, or to a lodge, or to a movie that no one else in the family wanted to see, have you ever stopped for a minute in front of your home to think of all that it holds that is close and irreplaceable? Sure, the place is kind of rundown; the steps need fixing, the chimney has to be rebuilt, a wrangle over new wallpaper clouds the horizon. Maybe you seesawed both sides of the headpin all night, forgot your lines at the installation of the Grand Master, or found the evening wasted on a movie that the rest of the family was smart enough to pass by. But for just a few seconds, imagine yourself a stranger on the outside.

That hammering down cellar comes from a boy who's building a soap box derby racer. Beneath the upstairs light, a girl is busy at her homework. The woman you can see through the living room window is practicing the piano because she gets sharps and flats mixed up and likes to play when no one — especially her husband — is listening.

To make it look inviting, we sometimes have to stand outside the shade of the family tree. There are days when any of us feels hedged in, held back and burdened by a family. But there are times — and one of them is when we're on the outside looking in — that we feel buoyed up, supported and helped because we know we can never be quite alone.

We've wondered if youngsters are ever fully aware of how much they contribute to the solidarity of the home — or if they ever feel responsible for easing family tensions. It's easy for parents to lose their balance when they're traveling the straight and narrow path. It's like trying to walk a rail. They can go a long way if a child just supports their hand.

We've read that it's good to think of your job — if it gets out of focus — from an imaginary vantage point 10,000 feet in the air. A pause before you touch the first step on the front porch helps to bring your home into perspective. A few seconds outside the circle deepens your appreciation for being the one who holds the pass key to the most important organization on earth — the family.

Listen, House!

I am the master here,

Not you.

I'm the king.

(At least that's what people always say.)

I will not be your obedient servant,

You hipped-roof hypochondriac.

Don't groan every time

Someone opens the door.

Put up a braver front to rainstorms.

Buck up against a good blow.

Get a hold of yourself,

Show a little spirit,

A little determination

To hold together.

I'll not pay much attention to you —

That's the Queen's province.

You say you don't see well . . . .

You need new glasses?

I rather like you the way you are.

If these full-view arrangements

Ever appeal to me

I shall abandon you altogether

And live in a pavilion.

Complaints annoy me.

You're feverish in summer,

Chilly in winter.

You'd like an amputation

Performed on the south porch.

Your elimination would be improved

By a garbage disposal unit.

I think you'd like your guts taken out

Just so you could talk about the operation.

Sometimes, House, I suspect that

You and the Queen are in cahoots.

I like you

When you don't get in the way.

But if I so much as restore one cell

You howl for a complete overhaul

Because nothing else matches.

You flaunt shabbiness

Like a beggar.

I am resolved now

Never to take that first step.

You worry me, House;

I'm uneasy on the throne.

When I had you paid for
I thought you'd be a free hold
To do with as I wanted.
Subservient? You?
You and The Cross — made of wood —
Burdens.

All I ask is that you
Protect me,
Support me,
Comfort me.
And don't go over my head
Or behind my back
To the Queen.

Remember, House,
I can always set fire to you
And go live in a tent.

There are people who get up at dawn to go on bird walks. I can swear to this because I married one of them. This feverish interest in winged whatnots is chronic — an infection that lasts a lifetime and breaks out in a rash every spring. It is a wholesome, healthy, harmless interest, but just a little baffling to one who was created without much natural curiosity into the chirpings, the colorings, the comings and goings of ruby-crowned kinglets, Maryland yellow-throats, rose-breasted grosbeaks or twitterpated bundigoes.

One thing all bird lovers have in common — they're never at a loss for a name. My own knowledge extends to crows, robins, and pigeons. I used to say sparrows but there are so many kinds of sparrows, I've excluded them from my field. If Marion says, "That's a red-eyed vireo," I'm in no position to dispute her any more than she is me when I hear an old record and tell her "that's Red Norvo with the old Goodman band."

Perhaps you've never been exposed to the companionship of an ornithologist. It's like this. You're hurrying along the street to get to a meeting. Your bird-conscious friend suddenly grips your arm and commands, "Wait," in a tone of voice that leads you to believe a cobra will strike if you take another step. You wait in enforced silence. "Hear it?" your companion says. You've heard an anonymous tweeting. "That's a Maryland yellow-throat . . . it says witchery . . .witchery . . . witchery." (People are always putting words in birds' mouths. The ruby-crowned kinglet is supposed to say, tee . . .tee . . . tee . . .tew . . . tew . . .tew . . . tidadee . . . tidadee . . . tidadee. But I don't think he would own up to uttering such nonsense.) You start to move on but the hand on your arm signals, "Not yet." You must accustom yourself to this. Bird watchers are always signaling non-bird-watchers: "Not yet."

Once, in a weak moment, I admit to pretending an interest in ornithology. It was the only way I ever knew to have a date with my girl at half-past five in the morning. It was a very satisfying arrangement. She watched the birds, I watched the girl. Later, of course, the deception was dropped. "If you can tell Vido Musso's tenor from Georgie Auld's or Arthur Rollini's, why can't you tell a peewee from a chickadee or a phoebe?" Marion would ask. "What note do you add to a C major seventh chord to make it a major ninth?" I would ask her right back and consider it a draw — which is about all any husband can hope for.

One Saturday noon when I came home from work, Marion met me at the corner of our lot and took my hand as if I were a little boy in kindergarten. When she is in the mood to play games, I humor her. She had her field glasses with her and she said very quietly, "Let's sit on the lawn and watch birds for a minute." Marion goes impractical on me every once in a while. "It's been wonderful out here this morning," she told me. "A wren looked over the bird house you made me and an oriole is working on that old nest in the elm tree." "No pie for lunch," I thought and obediently sat down on the ground.

The entertainment started immediately. She pointed out a white-crowned sparrow singing sweet nothings to nobody in particular. True male that he was, he left off his unappreciated warblings and came down on the lawn to look for something to eat. He hopped in a circle so I could see the stripes on his head — like the markings on football helmets that help the passer spot an end when he's downfield. I had to admire this dapper little bird. At least he was eating. He twittered happily and helped himself to lunch. To unearth hors d'oeuvres he jumped forward, then back with both feet in a quick motion like one of the Charleston steps. Nobody joined him for lunch so he flew off to happier hunting.

A half dozen goldfinches, a brilliant flying circus, darted across the lawn. They hovered over the barberry hedge and lit in the chokecherry tree. The males were dressed to kill — yellow sport jackets piped with black. Boy goldfinches have the right approach to girl goldfinches. Dazzle 'Em! How come us men abandoned such obvious tactics?

Things got dull and the ground got hard. We finally started for the house — a move in the right direction — I was hungry. When we reached the steps I noticed that no pie was cooling on the back porch. My hand was on the screen door when Marion gave me the bird watcher's "Stop, Look, and Listen" signal. "There's a flicker in the elm tree," she whispered. I prepared to watch with about as much interest as a woman at a burlesque show. But say, this flicker had things on his mind. He was intent on attracting a female. We couldn't see his femme fatale but she must have been a winged Ava Gardner. He stretched his neck, turned his head from side to side, writhed, shook, pleaded with a passion I little suspected flamed in a flicker's heart. He was a feathered Johnny Ray and I swear he laid right down on that limb and cried. I didn't know birds had to put up with this sort of thing. Well, the noon hour wasn't a total loss. To my meager list of robins, crows, and pigeons, I added a name. I can now tell a flicker when I see one.

No male likes to see another male get pushed around by the female of the species. My Friend Flicker was probably too preoccupied to notice, but if he had looked in our kitchen window, he would have seen that for Saturday lunch there was no pie. In spring, a bird watcher's pie is flying around in the sky.

This past summer, I made a feeble attempt at learning to play golf in the Corona Twilight League. My experience was somewhat limited, but I stayed with the game long enough to discover that the most valuable wood was not the driver or the number two, three or four wood. It was a pencil. I learned this the hard way. In order to keep my score straight, I put a handful of pennies in one pocket, and on every stroke I would change a penny from that pocket to another. I was extremely conscientious about not cheating, but one member of my team who saw me counting my money every few minutes on the course misunderstood. He drew me to one side and said, "If you haven't got enough dough to pay the green fees, I can lend you a couple of bucks until Friday." Since I didn't want to seem unduly worried about the cost of the game, I stopped using pennies and adopted another scoring device not unknown on golf courses generally. This is the "almost-as-good-as" technique. If my opponent said, "Give me an eight," I immediately responded with, "Put me down for a nine." If he said, "Six," I said, "Seven." These figures had no relation to the actual score, but since I let him take every hole anyway, he had no great complaint to make. Meanwhile, I attempted noon-hour practices with Carlon Tarbell and Bus Collier and read Ben Hogan's "Power Golf," but nothing was quite so effective in lowering my score as the "almost-as-good-as" technique, plus the compliant pencil.

The next logical step was to go on to the "anything-you-can-do-I-can-do-better-I-can-do-anything-better-than-you" method of scoring. This worked like a charm the first few holes. My opponent said, "Eight," so I said, "Seven."

He said, "Six."

I said, "Five."

He said, "Four!"

I said, "Three!"

He said, "TWO!"

"ONE," I said. "ONE MORE HOLE IS GOING TO MAKE AN AWFUL LIAR OUT OF SOMEBODY!"

So I went honest again. I got out my pennies and counted religiously. But I hadn't reckoned with the automatic-computer type of opponent. I reached for my pennies at the end of the first hole, counted them and said, not too proudly, "Thirteen." "No," stormed my opposite number, "You got fourteen." I nodded meek agreement to the scorekeeper. At the next hole I timidly announced, "Eleven." Recounting my progress stroke by stroke, my nemesis proved that it should be twelve. I took my pennies and threw them in the pond to keep company with several golf balls which had preceded them and played the next hole without bothering to keep any score at all. When we had all holed in, I turned to my opponent and said, helplessly, "I've lost count. How many did I get?" "How the hell should I know?" he roared indignantly, "Keep track of your own score."

This seemed like an impossible job so I gave up golf and returned to my first love, croquet. Nobody gets up early in the morning to play croquet. Only one club is needed, and the opportunities for cheating are about equal. I never fully appreciated what golf does to people until I heard a relieved wife say, "Mac is so grateful to be able to go to work on Monday morning. It takes his mind off his game."

Gerald in his fierce croquet stance, 1953

In common with most people, we feel inadequate in the face of many of the challenges we have to meet day after day. Most problems have no quick, easy solution. Many of them have no solution at all. The days when something was either yes or no, black or white, have gone. All we have left is the uneasy, fallible feeling of having said an equivocal "yes" when we should have said a hesitant "no." We feel an extravagant elation to have faced and solved a minor problem.

As in most discoveries, an element of good luck entered into the solution. But no inventor or scientist ever turned his back on an answer simply because it was accidentally arrived at. We have solved the pet problem. If you are now struggling with dogs, cats, canaries, horses, white mice, or parakeets, we have words of wisdom for you.

Our boyhood experience included caring for a runt pig, a stunted calf, a billy goat, numerous dogs and cats, snapping turtles, and pigeons. As a family man, a parallel procedure was gone through for the children. A tremendous expenditure of time — not begrudged, of course — but not to be born lightly either.

The archetype of all the pets who ever owned us was a large, liver and white Springer Spaniel named "Nicky." Nick would get us out of bed early Sunday morning when we wanted to sleep. Once outdoors he would bark to let man and beast know that he was up and doing. We were never able to get him to come back in and be quiet. He embarrassed us, defied us, inconvenienced us, outsmarted us, and made us love him deeply all at the same time. We haven't had much luck with dogs since. Besides, we can't offer a dog very much companionship in a house that's empty most of the time. Several weekly visits from "Speed," Otto Sandwick's little dachshund, keeps us in touch with the dog world. "Speed" entertains us then slips out of the house without any demands on us.

We never had any luck with cats. They never caught on to the niceties of existence with humans and we were relieved when they disappeared — sometimes through our own connivance. We had a fine relationship, again, on a strictly neighborly basis with George and Frances Pope's cat, "Zipper," who was every inch a gentleman and an individual — a requirement for any pet.

We were mastered for a while by a pigeon that Dave winged with his BB gun. In a contradictory expression of humanity — after he was inhuman enough to shoot the bird — Dave brought the pigeon home and nursed it back to health. We named him "Walter" and he had delusions of grandeur. You could shuffle up to him in a prize fighter's stance and Walter would ruffle his feathers, feint with his right and clip you on the leg with a sharp jab of his left wing. He was so belligerent that he believed in biting the hand that fed him. Walter was downright funny until he got to be nothing less than a damned nuisance — any of the neighbors will freely testify to this. The day he flew away to conquer the world was a happy one. We've always been surprised not to have heard that he had attacked and forced down a B-51. But enough time has passed so we've finally outgrown the fear that he would return.

This overlong recital is not without its point. Once a man has had a pet, he needs the satisfaction of being greeted at the door by, say, an excited dog — particularly if the dog is the only creature in the house happy to see him. But without pets, he is aware of a lightening of burdens — no licensing, no vet fees, no apologizing to neighbors. How to have the undeniable satisfaction without the interminable bother? — that is the problem that the perfect pet poses.

We have the answer — Crickets!

We can't recall what good fortune brought a pair of crickets to our hearth (we don't have a hearth but it's a pleasant fiction we're going to maintain for the cricket's sake). Ideally, crickets sing and live around the stones of a fireplace hearth, but our pair make themselves radiantly happy in the cellar. Modern crickets, you see, are asked to adjust to new situations and they do it beautifully. We suspect that our crickets were an overflow from a kindergarten project which is as good an explanation as any of the fortuitous accidents we mentioned at the outset.

Now every time the oil burner clicks on, the crickets sing their cozy autumnal song and since we're three months behind on our oil bill, we find it consoling to have someone in the house happy while more and more of our money goes up the chimney.

We mentioned, offhand, to a feminine friend of ours that we had crickets, Lillian and Merton, in the cellar and she reacted as violently as if we'd said we had cockroaches in the kitchen. She seemed revolted at the idea of being on friendly terms with the insect world. There are unsuspected advantages. Lately, we have noticed a decided trend toward temperance in our guests. Once a man hears — or thinks he hears — crickets, he looks quizzically at his tall glass and decides he has had enough.

Crickets, of course, don't have to be housebroken. They don't even have to be fed much — a piece of apple every two weeks. Or licensed. No booster shots. No late evening walks. No worming, delousing, no tracking up the porches, no pushing in or out of the screen door, no chasing motorcycles, or nipping the mailman. Crickets make absolutely no demands and yet they give a home that sense of well being and warmth which any pet worth having should produce.

Being something of a visionary, we foresee this country swept by a great wave of cricket ownership. We've got a head start in this business and we're devoting all our spare time to breeding a tough, happy, responsible line of crickets which will be in as great demand as cocker spaniels, parakeets, tropical fish or Siamese cats.

We shall be happy to put you on our waiting list.

David Fisher, bass; Gerald, vibes; and Lewis Robinson, guitar; 1952

Once or twice a month we push open the kitchen
door at 2 o'clock in the morning. We're thoroughly
tired after playing for a dance and happy to be off the
highway and home again. We rather enjoy playing on
a once-in-a-while basis. Over the years we've been in
some interesting places we never would have reached
otherwise.

We remember one Christmas season when we had
been laid low with a cold. We debated all day Friday
whether or not to play in Syracuse with Spiegle
Willcox. At the last minute we decided to go. When
we pushed the vibes onto the tenth floor of the hotel,
the ballroom had been transformed into an ice palace
for a party in honor of Betty Jane Marcellus. The
band was placed in a winter scene worthy of a

Hollywood musical. We made a complete recovery from our malaise at intermission over a steak and champagne supper.

At the other end of the social scale, but not the musical, we've never forgotten a job near Truxton with Larry Harrington. We played all night in a declasse joint with scarcely a listener except the manager. About ten minutes before closing, some Truxton muscle men moved in on the place looking for excitement. They gave everybody in the band — all four of us — a hard time. Being out-manned and out-muscled, we were careful not to answer back. Our retreat in the face of that drunken demolition gang was a tactical maneuver we would hate to attempt again.

A big cross section of life moves in front of a band — teenagers dancing in a millionaire's boathouse, bankers singing exuberantly and most unconservatively at the country club, seventh graders making their first attempt on the dance floor, a gray-haired couple waltzing on their anniversary . . . . and there's always the man who turns up with somebody else's wife who is surprised to find YOU playing in the band.

Recently we played in Ithaca at the Kappa Sigma fraternity. It was a thoroughly enjoyable experience. What is more pleasant than watching young men and women having a good time? The life of the party wasn't centered around the bar. There were a hundred wholesome collegians behaving pretty much as they would in their own homes. As always, we were tired when we reached our kitchen door, but we felt reassured, too, about the "coming generation", privileged to have watched them and pleased that the vibes had given us entree into another pleasant experience.

Some time ago I browbeat the rest of the family into letting me have a room to myself. It is a small room with bold green plaid wallpaper, a firm-mattressed bunk for taking naps, and a bulletin board for clippings and unanswered letters. There is also a gay-nineties revolving bookcase and a not-large-enough wastepaper basket.

I've never had a desk, and I don't want one. Instead, I've grown attached to a drop-leaf cherry table that Marion's father gave us. Like so many pieces that were made 75 or 100 years ago, this one had been subjected to several coats of red paint. Lew Beames gave me a hand in refinishing it. That, and the long hours spent scraping, sanding, varnishing, and rubbing, make the table more meaningful to me than any desk I might ever own. On the table, among other things, is the ancient and honorable Corona, vintage 1930.

The truth is that in this little room are all the things anyone needs to write. If you've ever thought that having a congenial place to yourself is all that you need to launch your Great American Novel, don't further disillusion yourself. It is what you bring into the room that is significant. I haven't brought any such ambitious project into my den. To write what is called a "good letter" seems to me to be a skill worth cultivating. I find a lot of satisfaction in writing for someone else what he hesitates to write for himself. There is some value in the self-imposed discipline of writing a column a week. At the very least, it keeps me in trim for the other outlets which turn up for anyone who can string words together in fairly palatable fashion.

In all honesty, this introspective mood came over me because of an unusual circumstance. The top of my cherry table is a no-woman's land piled high with clippings, magazines, half-read books, scribbled notes, and more pencils than an educated centipede would require. Tonight when I walked into the room, the table was cleared. For the first time in months I saw the well-remembered patterns in the grain of the wood. I wish my words could match their mellowness and beauty.

I remember that once I was a messenger for a Christmas Angel. It is strange that I could ever have forgotten it. As I wandered through the stores last weekend, I found it hard to summon forth the least bit of Christmas spirit. Perhaps it was the fact that my pocketbook wasn't equal to the occasion. More than that, I'm sure, was the feeling that what all of us need most for Christmas cannot be wrapped up in a package.

I should have remembered my Christmas journey as I went through the department stores and dress shops, the five and tens and bookstores. Curiously enough, the whole story came back to me as I read a wonderfully perceptive editorial in the Sunday *Times* written for "The 100 Neediest Cases."

"The neediest cases of today," said *The Times*, "are not the ragged children, the unemployed men, the starving . . . We who want to help the neediest must dig a little deeper. Not only into our pockets but also into the substance of human lives. It is easy to supply food and clothes and shelter; it is not so easy to supply expert guidance and practical advice to a distracted mother or a disturbed child . . . Needs change; methods of administering those needs change, too. What does not change and never will change is man's realization that he is his brother's keeper and that he can never divest himself of that responsibility so long as he lives."

I folded the paper in my lap and the picture of my Christmas Angel came to me full and clear. There was nothing ethereal about her. She was as sturdy as a pair of concrete steps. But there was nothing heavy and plodding about her, either. I guess she was more cherubic than angelic. Her eyes really twinkled like Santa Claus' are supposed to. She had a ready chuckle. In an offhand, completely unselfconscious way she bubbled with great good spirits.

You may have known her as Elizabeth Hugg. I always thought of that as an earthly alias. To my family she was known as "Hugg." I don't want to give the impression that she came alive to the blessings and responsibilities of life just before the presents are opened on Christmas. Hugg's radiance shone the year 'round. At Christmastime she just glowed a little brighter. In the late twenties and early thirties, Hugg was a county nurse, and she brought to her work that expert guidance and practical advice which The Times recognizes as being so important now. Hugg used to stop at my mother's house in those days. She often stayed for dinner, and it seemed as though we were always having Spanish rice, a filling but somewhat uninspired dish that tasted better on the days when Hugg came.

Christmas must have been a particularly busy time. I remember her dashing into the house one Saturday afternoon a few days before the great event. All she had time for was a quick "Hello" and a cup of coffee. As she started back to her car, she stopped suddenly to ask me if I'd help her out by carrying two baskets to one of her families. I readily agreed, but not from any noble motives. My mother stood behind me, and I knew that to refuse Hugg would only call maternal wrath on me and I'd have to deliver them anyway.

I took the two baskets. They were heavy, loaded with fresh fruit, cans of food and a few small toys attractively arranged around the top. I had the feeling, even then, that Hugg had at least matched the county's contribution out of her own pay, but I wasn't particularly moved at the start of this little errand of mercy. To help pass the time and to ease the burden of the baskets, I indulged in my own Christmas fancies. A 14-year-old boy can still conjure up magnificent dreams of things he knows he is not going to get.

My destination was a house set off by itself on a side street. It looked cold and dreary, drab and unprotected. No trees sheltered it. It stood alone, untended. What curtains there were at the windows were shabby enough to impress a boy who was never particularly conscious of such matters. A few pasteboard cartons had been tacked around the cellar wall to keep out the cold, but they only seemed to heighten the inadequacy of the house against the winds that whipped down the road.

I sat the baskets down frequently and changed hands with them. They were equally heavy, but when I picked them up again and started for the house I felt relieved from having shifted the weight. Suddenly I saw children at one of the windows. They had pushed the dirty curtains aside and watched me as I approached. The instant they were certain that I was coming to their house, they beat on the window and screamed and jumped up and down. I was astonished at all the excitement over two baskets of groceries and a few five-and-ten-cent toys. But I straightened up. The baskets became lighter. I hurried toward the house. The shouts of those children cracked the tough wall of selfishness a boy erects around himself.

When I neared the porch, the children abandoned their window and came screaming to the front door. They yanked the door open and suddenly, awed by the opulence of two whole baskets full of gifts, became quiet. A tired, haggard mother appeared. She smiled and pushed a broken chair out of the way so I could get into the hall. The children remained quiet. I wish that I had reached in my pocket and found something there — a quarter, a jackknife, anything — to have added to those two baskets. But I was so overcome that all I could say was "Hugg" and dropped the baskets in the hall and left.

As soon as I was off the porch, the children started screaming again, and it seemed to me I could hear them all the way home. I don't remember what I got for Christmas that year, but I know I was content with whatever it was. I felt the warmth of the reflected glow of someone else's benefactions.

That family has grown up now. Their very existence is a tribute to the skill of a county nurse who knew how to nurture soul and body, all seasons, year in and year out, unprompted by anything but the highest sense of duty.

In these days of relative plenty, there are still kids looking out of shabby windows — ask your pastor or your school nurse — with problems more complicated than they were in those Spanish rice days. Hard to get close to the real spirit of Christmas? It will help me if I can only remember that I was once messenger boy for a Christmas Angel.

Sometimes our village organist has musical delusions of grandeur. She gets carried away by the importance of the big sounds blasting out of the pipes. Likewise, this village columnist, swelled by the uncritical comments of two or three sweet old ladies, gets to thinking he, too, is making beautiful music. Then there are weeks when he feels like a fool for writing at all.

The truth, when he occasionally faces up to it, is that his town needs him — just as the church needs the organist even though she can't play Grade Four music. There are too many homes breaking up; there is labor trouble at the factory; there is an annual reminder to be written at Christmas that the Three Wise Men were not following a dollar sign in the sky. What if the local columnist isn't an Ernie Pyle? The need is there to observe and think and write with all the understanding and compassion he has. And some weeks he comes close — close to sounding the right note.

Reflections from His Wife

Gerald isn't feeling very well this week. He is afflicted by this mid-winter malaise when there is something to do. At the moment, the something to do is write the column and he just doesn't feel up to it.

We've been invited, half-heartedly we thought, to write the column before. But, at the last moment, he has always found excuses to do it himself.

Gerald is a model husband. I think he must be because there are so many more like him. In the kitchen he puts the dishes away and slams the cupboard doors and gives the impression that he has just cleaned the whole house.

Why should a man whose vacation included a look at some of the finest antique furniture at Winterthur in Wilmington, a glimpse of the New Frontier in Washington, and a few days in New York City for concerts and shows, be so impressed with a walk down an abandoned country road in Summer Hill?

Near sunset on a Saturday afternoon he stopped the car in front of a scrub apple tree with limbs crossed in a bizarre tangle. His eyes, accustomed to town sights, were not trained to recognize turtle-head blossoms and Joe-pye weed. But the eyes of his companion greeted old friends cultivated during a life-long acquaintance with nature. His ears were not attuned to the stereo music that crickets, toads and birds performed in concert on either side of the road. Program notes — "That's a thrush," or, "Listen to the killdeer scolding" — were freely supplied. The colors that filtered through his eccentric visual system he knew were brilliant to his companion. He could see acres of his own special version of browns and greens. The yellow of the goldenrod and the blue of the wild aster were easily identifiable. The tiny, knubby red astricans required special pointing out. And the sunset described to him as being all shades of oranges and yellows looked like the swirls of yellow an adventurous kindergartner might finger paint on a blue background.

There was not a single adventure on the entire walk. A cricket racing down a dusty rut was temporarily appropriated for a cricket cage in the Freeville Kindergarten. And a jay-walking toad was detained for a similar purpose. No deer in sight. No rabbits. An unwary young woodcock drank out of a roadside puddle, blinked in disbelief and flashed away when two curious, long-legged creatures advanced on him.

What was impressive then? The openness was impressive and the tempo. "We have time up here," the trees and grasses testified matter-of-factly. "Let us be and we will have this country beautiful again."

"Look up. Look off and up," the horizon invited. And a man accustomed to walking with his head down looked off and up easily and naturally. There in the sky with the yellow swirls were vapor trails. Far off, a jet sounded like an express train. The filmy underscore left by the jet emphasized how small a mark man makes on the universe even when he travels at twice the speed of sound. And among the trees that had been growing for thirty, fifty, one hundred years, the plane's journey seemed no more important than the woodcock's.

Perhaps a man can make too much of a walk down a lonely road. If he is looking for something to write, he might be suspected of squeezing a half dozen paragraphs out of the countryside. But he cannot fool himself or very many people about how he feels inside.

He finished his walk at the point where he started and stared again at the twisted limbs of the scrub apple. He remembered then how he felt when a tailor looked at him. "What can we do about the shoulders?" The tailor muttered behind his back to the salesman. And a man felt a kinship to a scrub apple tree. He felt the toughness to be what he must be. "You don't have to do anything about the shoulders," he had said.

He and his companion drove slowly back to town. The cricket and toad were carefully enclosed in gentle hands. After they had served as unwilling but lively instructors in the wonders of nature, they would be allowed to resume their interrupted journeys.

Not many answers are found on abandoned roads. A quiet walk at least helps a man to look knowingly at the new road he chooses — or is forced to choose. Most of all he gains — better than he can in Wilmington or Washington or New York — a perspective of his own importance and unimportance in the world in which he lives.

An amateur clown does not have to be funny when he doesn't feel like it. But the professional clown, heartbreak or no, must go on and wring the laughs out of his audience. The amateur musician can pick up or put down his fiddle as the mood strikes him. And so a man who likes to write for his own pleasure does not have to evoke Christmas in July or get a Thanksgiving piece out of his typewriter by Decoration Day. Although he may be denied the luxury of a check in the mail, he can indulge himself in the pleasure of thinking and writing about Labor Day on Labor Day.

To start such a day a man drives out of town early in the morning to a quiet country road. When he gets out of the car, pine trees thirty feet high stand on his right. To his left, open fields slope away to a view of the valley, an encircling range of hills, and still another range of hills beyond. As he walks slowly down the road, the wind stirs the pines to a freight-train-like roar. He turns off the road and enters an open lane into the woods. Maple trees shake their leaves in the wind with the high-pitched sizzle of a giant sheet of aluminum foil.

A man stands and listens and thinks. Labor Day is a time to walk away from his job and look back at it over his shoulder — to review his work life and its importance to him. A man who has painted hundreds of windows, shoveled crushed stone, mowed roadsides with a scythe, and assembled and inspected typewriters, isn't thinking about work in academic terms. He remembers blisters on his hands, an aching back, boredom, frustration. But from the vantage point of two score and ten, he sees that work, any kind of work, every kind of work, has been his salvation.

Save for the chirping of a few crickets, there is no other sound. He looks at the quiet pine trees rooted in orderly ranks. Their job is to stand in one place and grow; their assignment clear cut; their strength and massed beauty, their silent and sturdy companionship reassuring.

As he turns the corner to start the third leg of his journey, a partridge takes off from the underbrush with such a throbbing commotion that a man is startled out of his reflective mood. He walks along a grassy lane now. The dew is heavy and he feels the damp coolness. What about the work, the plain, hard work, a man asks himself, that must get done each day? Is there anything ennobling about tending a bread wrapping machine, driving a truck, or putting a typewriter together? A man can only answer for himself. Without work, for all the problems it creates, his life would largely be meaningless.

As he reaches the end of the grassy lane, a man concludes that if he could somehow have been supported through the years without having to work he would long ago have destroyed himself. The compulsion to get out of bed and labor was as necessary for him as eating and breathing. To have the right job may be ideal — only a few men manage this — to have a job is cause for gratitude on this particular holiday.

As he makes the final turn of this morning's walk, a man falls easily into a path worn by tractors and wagons. He finds himself suddenly kicking through curled and dried linden leaves. And he catches, in mid-air, a leaf gracefully slipping to the ground; a reminder, he tells himself, to be with nature flexible and adaptable, a man for all seasons.

At the end of his walk, the pine trees frame again the sweeping view across alfalfa and corn fields into the valley and up to the hills. A man stops and looks into the distance. He smiles broadly to himself and remembers the latest bit of family news. His grandson has a tooth now, a tooth to click proudly on the edge of his cup. On Labor Day what more could a man wish his grandson, than that he may know the discipline and satisfaction of work, hard work and, in his own time, the pleasure of a quiet, reflective walk on a beautiful Labor Day morning.

What does a man think about when he moves from a plant where he has worked for nearly 30 years. He certainly thinks about the first day he came to work. It was a hot summer afternoon in 1929. In the morning he had been hanging around Pete Hoffman's combination pool room and barber shop taking lessons in nine ball. Mr. C.D. Corwin, the Works Manager of the Smith-Corona plant, came in to get a haircut. When he got out of the barber chair, Mr. Corwin recommended quite directly reporting at one o'clock for a painting job with the millwrights. At one o'clock pool cue was exchanged for paint brush and a stringy young man was high on a platform painting the ceiling of a hot steamy plating room.

After that there were many jobs; painting window sashes from a scaffold, soldering Model Three typewriters, adjusting, final inspection, parts inspections, tool inspections, and finally, personnel. All the years tumble together and a man thinks about learning to read "mikes"; of arguing over a fraction of a millimeter as if it were as big as a half-acre; of waking in the middle of the night and turning over possibility after possibility in an effort to come to a good decision.

A man may ask himself in all honesty why he did these things. He worked for money, of course. It was essential; it was appreciated. More than that, he became involved in the fascinating enterprise of making typewriters and he has no regret for his involvement.

$^\jmath$micrometers - used to measure parts in millimeters

So many things are insincerely said that words have been robbed of nearly all meaning. When the time comes to put down an exact and honest feeling, the true must be suspected of being merely polite. A man can only say that when he looked out his office window to watch the men and women in the plant go home at night, he felt a warmth toward them, an identification with them that was deep and open and honest. He knows, too, that he is not alone in this feeling. And he is puzzled by the desperate attempts all of us make to cross a bridge that in reality does not exist.

A man thinks, too, that he must not look backward. Life by its very terms must be lived through change. However, as much as a man tells himself these things, he cannot escape the inner wrench when he turns from what has been a part of him for too long a time. He is not disturbed by new ways or new assignments. He has said to others — and to himself — that we have more to look forward to than to look back on.

Nevertheless, he cannot prevent himself from looking down the long years; the hard days forgotten; the disappointments blunted by time; the disagreements softened; the mistakes that were not correctable, lived through and learned from. He feels deeply how much of him is left in a typewriter plant that holds a thousand-and-one never-to-be-told stories.

A man who has already savored the challenge of a new assignment and finds it to his liking takes a hopeful look forward, a fond look back, and quietly puts another chapter of his life behind him.

"Let us speak honestly across the barrier"

Camus

"So you're back," my favorite tree said to me.

I stood there awkwardly in the rain. A cold wind rippled the water high in the ditches at the side of the road.

"I've thought about you often," I said uncomfortably.

"I suppose you have," came the diffident answer, "A lot has changed around here since your last visit."

"I noticed that the maples are gone," I said apologetically.

"Firewood," the tree answered. "There is some advantage in being a badly twisted scrub apple."

"Something about you impressed me from the very beginning," I put in lamely.

"You said that once before. Well, you're not alone. The road men have been eyeing me lately. A few bursts of their power saw would quickly convert me into an undistinguished pile of brush."

"Well, we all live on the brink these days . . . not that I want to talk about Cuba," I added quickly.

"Let us speak honestly across the barrier," the tree said, "that's a quote from Camus I've been saving up for you. It has been lonesome up here. A few hunters have gone by but they looked right through me without ever seeing whatever it is you see in me."

"I think I see myself," I said honestly. "I'm drawn to you because you're what you are for all to see."

"You mean men aren't like that," the tree said. "You don't look very complicated to me."

"I'm not very complicated," I said after awhile. "It's difficult to explain. I try hard to establish my separateness. At the same time I wonder how firm my links are with other men. I would like to let every person know how I feel; to give some reassurance that I know what it is to be lonely and un-listened to and

190

forgotten; that I know, too, what it is to be warmed by close human ties, to establish contact, to be remembered. Yet, how much can a man sustain for others and how much can he ask others to sustain for him?"

"I can tell you what it's like to be here in the winter," the tree said, "with only my topmost branches above the snow. I know what happens in the spring when the grasses come to life in the ditch and the sap starts flowing through my roots. I know bud and blossom, heat, wind and rains; the long summer. Fruit I know. And the fall, when you first found me, I understand well. But your answers are not in me. You cannot stand there and ask me for more than I know. You live like most men with a fear that is not incompatible with courage. You want a dialogue when most men do not want to talk. You want life to be clear and open when you would shrink from standing here at the road beside me and reveal yourself — your goodness and your ugliness. And even if you could, you would be embarrassingly lonely. I know only what nature has programmed me to know. Your problem is that you will not content yourself with such an answer."

I nodded my head in agreement and started to walk slowly away.

"Come back," my tree called after me. "I too need reassurance."

I turned and looked down the long road lined on either side by weeds and grasses, maple saplings, scraggly pines, and standing nearly alone, my strangely twisted scrub apple tree. The road was rutted and the ruts were filled with water. A bitter wind swept down the road and the water in the ruts shivered.

I nodded a promise and turned and walked away.

"Time is the great unknown

in the life equation, and

we're never quite prepared

for the unlikely day

when it finally equals zero."

— 1960 —

♪

About the author

Gerald was one of seven red-haired children of John and Margaret McCormick Barry. They were typical of the poor Irish Catholic families of the early 1900s. John was a laborer, mason, house painter, baker, cook, or launderer. Margaret was a washerwoman and house cleaner. The children helped their parents delivering laundry, gardening, and painting houses.

Gerald graduated from Groton High School in 1929, and his sweetheart, Marion McElheny, graduated in 1930. He attended Notre Dame for one year. She went to Cornell for 1½ years. They married in 1931 and lived with his parents. He worked on the town road crew when Margaret was born in 1932 and as a ceiling painter at Smith Corona in 1933 when David was born. He learned tool inspection and later became personnel director.

The Smith Corona typewriter plant on Main Street was the main employer for the town of 2,500 people. Groton considered itself "The Typewriter Capital of the World" and manufactured portable typewriters in the U.S. long after other typewriter companies had moved their operations oversees.

In his last years at SCM in Cortland, he was responsible for the *Keyboard*, the SCM newsletter, and for public relations. He produced and traveled with a three-projector slide show called "An Armchair Tour of Smith-Corona."

He began writing for publication in high school with a first story about the Groton High football loss to Cortland, Sept. 29, 1927. He did not include the score of the game but urged fans to come out in large numbers to cheer for their team at the next game. He wrote in all seasons through 1929. He was also as talented an athlete as several of his brothers but his sports participation was limited after he was diagnosed with rheumatic fever as an eighth grader. While he was bed-ridden, he taught himself to read music and play his sister's mandolin.

During his high school years he learned to play drums by watching older students perform. He assembled a make-shift set for himself. He was a member of the marching band at Notre Dame. During the Depression, he played drums in vaudeville shows in Cortland to supplement the family income. He took opportunities to discuss percussion techniques with many traveling musicians – Gene Krupa and Lionel Hampton, among them. Gerald had purchased a second hand vibraphone by then. (Vibraphones were unusual and under-appreciated instruments in the '30s.) He and Hampton exchanged ideas and their own hand made vibe mallets.

Gerald listened regularly to Adrian Rollini's Quartet (Rollini, vibes) radio broadcasts from New York City. He corresponded with Rollini and purchased some used percussion instruments from him. He learned many of Benny Goodman's arrangements (Red Norvo, vibes) and played well by ear but taught himself chord structure and arranging.

He started writing a weekly column, "Reflections," for *The Groton Journal and Courier* in 1949 and continued until the paper closed in the 1960s.

He was active in community activities, improving the library's access to service, raising money for a new town swimming pool, organizing a community orchestra and a community drama group, planning the development of the golf course and the community college.

He bought second-hand darkroom equipment when his first grandson was born in 1961. He called his first efforts "Grainy Photos Inc." but he became an increasingly proficient photographer. He used his studies of SCM workers in the *Keyboard* and photographed the participants at the Yeats Institute, Sligo, Ireland. He added color photography and developed beautiful prints in spite of his colorblindness and the poor temperature control on the old-fashioned cellar laundry tub faucets.

He worked vigorously for the founding of a community college in the area. When it opened in Groton he was finishing his public relations work at SCM in Cortland and beginning his "dream job" in public relations for the college. He died in an accident after his car skidded on a patch of ice as he made a final trip to Cortland.

♪

About the editor

In 1933, Mom and Dad's first home was a rented half-house at 105 Barrows Street. It had a coal furnace with one large circular register, a coal kitchen stove, an ice box, no telephone, and no car. A man with a horse and wagon delivered the coal in winter and ice in the summer.

In 1940 when we moved across the street to our own house at 110, we had a coal furnace with hot water radiators (the coal now came in a truck), an electric stove, refrigerator, party-line phone with a live operator, and in some years, a car. We did not use a house key. The house was always open to family, friends, neighbors, and kids.

Barrows Street was one large neighborhood playground. Each kid's house had a special attraction – a climbing tree, a back yard for kickball, a field for softball. Barrows Street was a long hill, ideal for sledding. The tiered pasture beside it was a heart-pounding ride if you dared start at the top by the well house.

The town was the larger playground – the school swings, Jones' Drug Store soda fountain, Pete's Place, and the Corona Baseball field. The first Sykes St. swimming pool was a dammed-up creek with cement sides. The mud bottom was an inspiration to learn swimming quickly. If you walked on the bottom, you got leeches on your legs!

At home we did our own papering, painting, carpentry, and yard work. We each had assignments for painting the house exterior. Dad painted the top of the north side on a long ladder, but we were able to do much of the second story from the roofs of the three porches. Those porches seemed to have hundreds of spindles. They were my additional job because I was "careful."

During World War II, we raised chickens for eggs and meat. We converted the croquet part of the back yard into a large Victory Garden. My brother or I walked down Barrows Street to a man with a few cows to buy unpastuerized milk in our own bottles.

The family budget was built for Comfort Foods. We ate creamed codfish (Gorton's in the wooden box later used for crayons and treasures), creamed chipped beef, eggs, potatoes, onions, carrots, or celery. Corn meal mush for Friday morning breakfast meant the treat of sliced, fried mush with maple syrup on Saturday morning. The mush was fried in bacon fat saved from the last batch.

Mom was serious about iron. We had liver once a week, raisins in oatmeal and in peanut butter sandwiches (no jelly), molasses on bread and butter, and molasses in milk (no chocolate). Worse, she brought puff-balls, mushrooms, or strange green things back from hikes. She did not get applause for her milkweed pod soup. She moved on to a wheat germ phase.

Drumming on the table was sometimes the lunch appetizer at our house. At noon, Dad walked home from Smith-Corona and my brother and I walked home from school. While Mom finished in the kitchen, we had a rhythm lesson with hands on the dining room table: march time, waltz time, off-beat, triplets, and even 3 over 2. (I did not take drum lessons and I gave up piano lessons in 8th grade, but the beat was planted. I started taking percussion lessons after I retired from teaching.)

Sometimes the pre-lunch activity was marching all over the house to "The Stars and Stripes Forever," the theme music for the National Farm and Home Hour radio broadcast. We learned that the left foot goes down on beats 1 and 3. The radio was also turned on for the news, classical music from WQXR in New York, live jazz, "Let's Pretend" on Saturday mornings, and for limited installments, "The Lone Ranger."

We were a family of readers and regular patrons of the Groton Library. When we were very small, Dad gave dramatic readings of the Sunday comics. My favorite was Oofty Goofty in "Alley Oop." Later we read aloud from humorous books: *The Pooh Library*, *Archie and Mehitabel*, and James Thurber stories. When we heated only the kitchen during WWII, Dad read (with Scottish accent) the serialized Glencannon stories from *The Saturday Evening Post* while we did the dishes.

My parents were dissimilar in temperament. Dad was a quiet, private person with a public role which he understood and valued. He was accepting of daily trials, but questioning of spiritual tribulations. He was deeply serious and disarmingly funny.

Mom was energetic, determined, and practical. She was an independent woman who wanted "to get things done." She loved teaching kindergarteners and that comes with its own special set of characteristics: patience, kindness, and endurance.

Mom loved the outdoors, Dad got sun poisoning. Dad loved to play music; Mom was not great on pitch or rhythm. They worked out their differences in a creative and loving way. Early in their marriage, they must have agreed on an atmosphere they wanted in their home. It was not one either had grown up with. They wanted a place of quiet for reading, music, conversation (not gossip), family activities, friends and fun. They balanced picnics and photography, bird walks and Boccherini, travel and staying home.

My parents were similar in their loving generosity and community activism. They had faith in people, self-improvement, and in hard work. For the factory and farm workers in Groton and for my family, hard work was a common denominator.

School seemed like hard work to me and I always carried all my books to give the impression of being a serious student. I was more confident in 7th grade with my first real job – a paper route. Girls were not allowed to have routes but the *Syracuse Herald* manager couldn't find a boy so I was "Mark" Barry with the promise that I wouldn't tell. For two summers I worked every day as a "mother's helper" for a woman with two baby boys.

In high school, my brother took the paper route and I cleaned houses and worked at a soda fountain. I helped clean barns in exchange for horseback riding lessons. I played piano for beginning ballet lessons in Helen Farrell's classes in exchange for my own dance lessons.

I worked for room and board at Cornell by training and supervising freshman waitresses. Cornell had formal dining room service called "gracious living" but

35 hours a week of gracious work didn't help my science labs or GPA.

After college graduation, I returned to Groton for the 1955 opening of the new school as a 7-9 science teacher. I survived the first week of teaching without chairs, lab desks, textbooks, or a voice (laryngitis). The students were good sports about "camping out" in the science lab..

A move to Rochester the next year didn't loosen ties to Groton. It has remained, through frequent visits, the place for family and friends and for reminders of why I am who I am.

 When I look back at my 1950 Groton yearbook, I cringe at the quote selected for me: "My joys are mingled with earnest occupation." It's quaint with no flair and no humor. But it's probably true.

I found great joy and more earnest occupation than I anticipated in publishing this book. I learned more about my family, my town, and myself in doing it. I am richer for the effort.

♪

My grandson, Griffin, (back cover) is the son of Lisa C. and Kris Schneider.

"My joys are mingled with earnest occupation."
Margaret Barry
Senior Photo
Groton Yearbook 1950

Please send "Reflections from a small town" to:

Name _____

Address _____

City_____ State____ Zip_____

Tel._____ e-mail _____

Book $15.00 each   _____

Sales tax   8% NYS   _____

Shipping $2.00 per book   _____

                Total   _____

Make checks payable to " Reflections – Gerald Barry"

Send to: Margaret Barry
             PO Box 18362
             Rochester, New York
             14618-0362

Please add questions, comments, or requests.

e-mail   magbarry@rochester.rr.com